TRUE SPIN

THE INDUSTRIAL MANAGER'S GUIDE
TO EFFECTIVE, HONEST PUBLIC
COMMUNICATIONS

TRUE SPIN

ANN S. GREEN

Advantage

Published by Advantage, Charleston, South Carolina.
Member of Advantage Media Group.

ADVANTAGE is a registered trademark, and the Advantage colophon is a trademark of Advantage Media Group, Inc.

Printed in the United States of America.

10 9 8 7 6 5 4 3 2 1

ISBN: 978-1-59932-841-6
LCCN: 2017939982

Cover design and layout by Katie Biondo.

This publication is designed to provide accurate and authoritative information in regard to the subject matter covered. It is sold with the understanding that the publisher is not engaged in rendering legal, accounting, or other professional services. If legal advice or other expert assistance is required, the services of a competent professional person should be sought.

Advantage Media Group is proud to be a part of the Tree Neutral® program. Tree Neutral offsets the number of trees consumed in the production and printing of this book by taking proactive steps such as planting trees in direct proportion to the number of trees used to print books. To learn more about Tree Neutral, please visit **www.treeneutral.com.**

Advantage Media Group is a publisher of business, self-improvement, and professional development books. We help entrepreneurs, business leaders, and professionals share their Stories, Passion, and Knowledge to help others Learn & Grow. Do you have a manuscript or book idea that you would like us to consider for publishing? Please visit **advantagefamily.com** or call **1.866.775.1696.**

To all the volunteers who have so graciously served on our community advisory panels over the years. Within these pages are many of your stories as well as my own. Thank you.

TABLE OF CONTENTS

Acknowledgments i

Introduction 1

Chapter One 7
IT'S ALL ABOUT CONTROL

Chapter Two 17
A LITTLE HISTORY

Chapter Three 25
PUBLIC PARTICIPATION IN THE
REGULATED INDUSTRIES

Chapter Four 35
UNDERSTANDING YOUR AUDIENCES

Chapter Five 51
EMBRACING THE PUBLIC PARTICIPATION PROCESS

Chapter Six 71
GETTING PERMISSION TO OPERATE

Chapter Seven 89
ENVIRONMENTAL JUSTICE

Chapter Eight 101
BUILDING SUSTAINABLE COMMUNITIES

Chapter Nine 109
PUBLIC ENGAGEMENT DURING A CRISIS

Conclusion 121
PUBLIC ENGAGEMENT IS THE NEWEST TECHNOLOGY

About the Author 127

About Ann Green Communications 129

Services 131

ACKNOWLEDGMENTS

To the first journalist I knew, my mother, Opal Vincent Starcher, whose memory still inspires me.

To Professor Emeritus Yvonne H. King, Glenville State College, whose firm direction balanced with words of encouragement still ring in my ears.

To my husband, Larry, whose confidence in me and unfailing love and support allowed me to follow my dream of creating Ann Green Communications.

INTRODUCTION

We arrived at the auditorium just before the public meeting was scheduled to begin. The anger in the room was palpable—startling, almost frightening. All eyes were on the three of us as we walked in: Robert Kennedy, the newly chosen president of Union Carbide Corporation; Thad Epps, the regional director of public affairs for Union Carbide; and me, their public relations consultant. Thad and I had worked with Mr. Kennedy for a couple of hours before the meeting in an effort to prepare him for this negative environment, but it was clear from the redness in his face and stiffness in his demeanor that we hadn't succeeded. Our coaching was in the traditional public relations (PR) mold. We had hoped an apology for the incident and commitment to operate safely in the future would do the trick. Traditional PR of the day was one-way messaging. Do what is needed to make the bad facts look as palatable as possible. Mr. Kennedy didn't lie to the audience that day, but he wasn't able to respond to their heartfelt fears because he didn't listen to them.

Mr. Kennedy took the podium to give his statement of apology for the release of a chemical used to make pesticides that had permeated the Institute, West Virginia, community on a beautiful August morning and sickened dozens of people. The Institute plant release was just eight months removed from the world's worst industrial accident ever, at the Union Carbide plant in Bhopal, India, which killed an estimated 2,500 people in 1984.

The Bhopal tragedy came as a shock to the world—but it was particularly disconcerting to the people of Institute. Residents of Institute had only recently learned that they lived in the shadow of the plant that housed the sister unit to the one that released the deadly gas in India.

The Institute plant had been a fixture in the community since the 1950s, when it was built by the government. The sprawling complex of brick administration buildings and the boilers and pipes of production units was situated along the Kanawha River nine miles from West Virginia's capital city, Charleston. It provided high-paying jobs to more than two thousand people, though not a lot of them came from the Institute community. Legend had it that in the plant's early days, young men clutching their newly earned degrees from neighboring West Virginia State College, a historically black college, would apply for management jobs only to be handed a broom.

I'd had close ties with the college in the past. In the early 1970s, I served as director of public relations and taught in the Communications Department. I formed many lifelong friendships during those years. This fact made what was to come all the more difficult. These relationships also helped shape my vision of True Spin.

Now, in 1985, we were attending a public meeting at this same college. The auditorium was filled. Most of the faces were familiar to us because of the public relations work we had done after Bhopal to reassure the community that what happened in India could not happen in the United States.

Logic told us that while the August incident in Institute was frightening and concerning, the fact was that it wasn't anything like Bhopal. What we had not understood was that "fact" meant little to the citizens who were affected by the release.

Follow-up questions from the audience made it clear that Mr. Kennedy's message was not well received. How could the plant have allowed a major release like this? How would exposure to the chemicals released affect the long-term health of the residents? Why weren't people forewarned about the dangers of the chemicals? Why weren't there emergency alerts to allow people to escape?

A young woman slowly stood and in an angry, quivering voice demanded that the plant be closed. Then she cried,

"I didn't bring my children into this world to have Union Carbide take them away." Clearly, this crowd wanted the plant to *go away*.

This was the moment I realized that where environmental, health, and safety issues are concerned, traditional public relations just doesn't cut it. In this moment, the trajectory of my career made a sharp turn.

The paradigm shift I experienced during that meeting in 1985 meant I could no longer help companies put the best face on bad situations. I couldn't make their bad facts look good. Further, I understood for the first time that any effort at spinning messages about the health and safety of people is not only morally wrong but *doesn't even work*. It led me to embrace a new brand of communications strategy and, ultimately, create Ann Green Communications. For the last quarter century, I've been committed to helping clients communicate candidly about their operations and listen to their stakeholders. Instead of PR spinning, I've come to call it "True Spin."

In the case of the Institute community, I recommended we bring community leaders and concerned citizens together to discuss the neighbors' fears of living next to a big chemical plant. The public meeting had felt like a trial; the dialogue sessions were civil and respectful. Without realizing it, I would build my career on the concept of small-group dialogue sessions like these.

Over the time since then, the citizens have worked with the plant to address many of the issues raised in those early days: safety concerns, development of emergency response notification systems, and an ongoing program of support from the plant to help sustain the community. To this day, my firm facilitates the continuing dialogue between current plant owners and citizens in the area to address their concerns and address community needs.

In the following pages, we will share some of the ways we've helped our clients build real and meaningful relationships with the people who live near their manufacturing facilities or remediation sites and help sustain the communities in which they operate.

I certainly couldn't do it alone. The entire team at Ann Green Communications has created the many solutions in our arsenal for breaking down walls and building real relationships, one community at time.

Trust is earned. But how can a chemical plant or refinery or mine or wind farm earn it? It's all about being credible—being "real." It's about listening even when the message isn't easy to hear. It's about ultimately caring about the people and the community in which you operate. It's about True Spin.

Before you decide this "touchy-feely" stuff is not for you, let me give you a pragmatic reason to continue. Engaging your stakeholders has real value to you. Allowing the public to become a legitimate partner with your operations will make advancing your initiatives a great deal easier. Your next permitting process will go more smoothly. You will be able to maintain good relationships with local elected officials with the least investment of time. You won't be spending tons of money on lawyers to defend against lawsuits from upset neighbors. You will be able to target your local philanthropy to make the most impact in the community with the fewest dollars. Your company will be perceived as a good place to work, so you will be able to recruit the best local talent. And if you adopt these philosophies, your career can soar.

In the coming pages, we will explore the history of the environmental movement and industry's response to it.

We will discuss how to share information with your neighbors and allow them to be partners in your operations—without giving up your autonomy.

We will help you better understand what the public wants and needs from the industries in their towns and identify ways to improve communications with your neighbors.

We will talk about challenges in the permitting process and ideas for meeting those challenges.

We will guide you in becoming a partner with the communities in which you operate and help you to sustain them over the long haul.

We will look at the emerging issue of environmental justice.

Finally, we will discuss public engagement during a crisis.

It's time to embrace True Spin at your organization to start building trusting relationships with the community. Let's get started.

CHAPTER ONE

It's All About Control

Y ou call your local auto repair shop to schedule an appointment for service—just an oil change. You get up early to get your car in the shop before work. When you arrive, the receptionist doesn't have you on the day's list. She can't work you in, either. The worst part—she doesn't seem to believe that you had an appointment or care that you have been inconvenienced. In fact, while not downright rude, she's definitely indifferent.

Something like this has happened to all of us at some time. We recall the feeling of frustration—even anger—that results. Although we did what we were supposed to do, we can't do a thing to make the others live up to their responsibility. We feel powerless. We feel a lack of control over that aspect of our lives.

These experiences can have physical consequences. When we become frustrated or angry, we may feel our blood pressure rise. Our temperature may also rise, and our heart rate quickens. Our voice may become louder or higher pitched. All of these are symptoms of increased adrenalin pulsing through our veins when confronted with an uncomfortable situation. It's the "fight or flight" response, and in the repair shop scenario, most of us would like to fight.

Now, instead of this common form of consumer complaint, imagine you are a parent who rushes a child to an emergency room only to get stonewalled in your efforts to acquire quick medical care for your little one. As time passes and your child becomes sicker, your level of frustration is fueled by fear. Add this dose of fear and dread to that frustration and you've put your physical reaction on steroids.

This is the sort of reaction that people living near an industrial operation might have during a release or environmental incident. They don't understand what has happened and how the material involved might affect them or their family, and they may not know what actions they should take to protect themselves. They feel helpless. As their frustration rises, their level of trust in those who may have caused their discomfort plummets.

Mistrust—it's the number-one result of lack of information in an emergency. Once people mistrust another person or entity, it's hard to regain their trust. Remember the old adage: "Fool me once, shame on you; fool me twice, shame on me." We humans are loathe to be made fools of, and we can hold onto resentment of those we feel have mistreated us for a long time. How likely would you be to go back to the auto repair shop where the attendant disrespected you?

Mistrust can lay dormant for years and manifest itself later—during, for example, a heated public hearing over an expansion permit. The talented team at Ann Green Communications and I have worked with hundreds of industrial companies all over the country to identify and then correct the source of that deep-seated mistrust. Our clients represent a variety of industries, from chemical to coal to cement to fertilizer to utilities. All face similar obstacles, and we have found that the solution lies in open, honest dialogue, or "True Spin."

Here's a common scenario. Company management wants to expand Plant A. The expansion will bring a few new jobs to the area and will help the company's bottom line. From a technical level, it's not a bad deal. It's not even particularly challenging from an environmental, health, and safety perspective. Regulators seem to think the permit application is in order. You've not had any significant issues for years. The permitting process should be a piece of cake. The managers go to the required public meeting led by the state regulators without much thought or preparation. But instead of the perfunctory meeting they expect, they are blindsided by a hostile crowd of neighbors opposing their plans.

Nothing prepared them for this, because they didn't have a relationship with their neighbors. They hadn't shared anything about their plans with the community. They had no idea of the latent concerns that residents had about their operations. They are surprised and befuddled.

How can plant management avoid such a situation? It's all about building credibility.

Neighbors who believe you are being honest and open with them are more likely to see you as credible. Credibility, the quality of being believable, is a fundamental precursor to trust—the belief that someone or something is reliable and honest. By delivering consistent value to stakeholders, you are perceived as credible—those stakeholders believe you will continue to provide good value. But you have to go the extra mile to earn those stakeholders' trust; you have to build relationships. Credibility comes first. So how do you build credibility?

Let's start with the fundamentals. Do we see as more credible the honest person who tells us how much they know or the honest person who makes an effort to understand us? For most people, it's about being listened to and being heard.

Think back to the frustrating experience in the auto shop scenario. How would you have felt if the person at the repair shop had stopped to listen and shown empathy instead of indifference? Wouldn't your level of frustration have been lessened?

Building credibility through listening is critical to building trust. Listening can be hard. If you are on the receiving end of unpleasant feedback on your operations, particularly with angry words and delivery, it's tough. If you don't believe the complainer's sentiments or you dislike the messenger, you can discount the message. But you do so at your own peril.

When people are frustrated, angry, or fearful, they want a situation resolved. They want to be taken seriously. They want to be treated with respect. They want immediate action and to have the problem corrected so that it never happens again. All of these things matter, but what people want most is to be listened to.

Listening to an emotionally charged neighbor is difficult. What they say may not even make sense to a highly trained engineer who makes decisions from the facts as they are presented. Such a person may be a good engineer but a bad listener.

Bad listening habits are easy to learn but hard to break. Let's review a few common ones.

If your neighbor doesn't deliver his or her message well, whether because of bad grammar or slang, it is easy to discount the message. You might be tempted to fake attention. You might listen only to the words being spoken but fail to "listen" for the feelings with which those words are conveyed.

What if someone delivers their message with profanity? Do you discount what they are trying to convey, or do you recognize that the profanity is illustrative of their frustration and anger?

Although most of us like to think we aren't prejudiced individuals, the reality is that biases and prejudices do exist and can interfere with our ability to listen. Beyond the most notable racial and ethnic prejudices, people may be biased against those who are different for any number of reasons. Someone has body art or piercings, or perhaps they don't speak English clearly or grammatically. These and similar biases can stand as blocks to hearing their messages. But these barriers to good listening can be overcome with the conviction of the listener that hearing the message is more important than anything else at that particular moment.

Effective listening, then, comes down to three basic steps: listen, question, and restate. Make sure you understand the message by taking in the words spoken to you, questioning whether you have heard the words correctly, and then restating the message in your own words to be certain you have understood. This process, called reflective listening, allows the listener to focus on the message and be sure that they fully understand it. It also allows the speaker to know that the listener is trying to understand and has, in fact, understood.

Focusing on the message—including the emotions with which it is delivered—and not any failings in the messenger, can mean the difference between successful communications and failure to connect and ultimately between success and failure in acquiring that permit or other goal.

The ability to listen is one piece in the puzzle of building solid relations with your stakeholders. Because you listen, you are signaling that you are willing to engage in a dialogue about the issue at hand. That brings us back to the notion that people want control over their lives and what is going on around them. Listening is the first step in building credibility. As we've said, being perceived as credible is the precursor to being trusted.

Whether they are your work team, neighbors, local elected officials, or shareholders, receiving the trust of your stakeholders is paramount in achieving your goals. The quickest way to be trusted is to share power.

Studies of worker satisfaction illustrate this point. When employees are told exactly how to do a task on the job, without being allowed to exercise personal creativity, they become dissatisfied with the work. It's boring, and it insults their intelligence. On the other hand, when employees are allowed to offer suggestions and be part of a team to accomplish a task, their level of satisfaction rises proportionately. That's why so many companies are moving toward collaborative workforces. Productivity is higher because the workers feel they have more control over their day and have more job satisfaction as a result.

The same theory applies to citizens living near facilities that can present a danger to the public if something goes wrong, such as those that handle hazardous materials. By allowing neighbors to have a dialogue with the local plant management—by having input into what goes on—their level of satisfaction rises. Just like the workers, they feel more in control of their environment. Knowledge, and the ability to have input in what affects them, gives citizens a sense of power. Powerlessness only leads to frustration, fear, and anger.

CONTROL

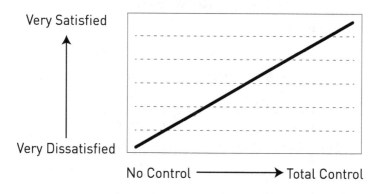

That satisfaction is directly proportional to the amount of control stakeholders feel. The more information stakeholders are given and understand, and the more they are allowed to give input on that information, the more likely they are to feel satisfied. This isn't a ruse to gain support. Rather, the sharing of information to gain satisfaction from the listener, and the willingness to hear their response to that information, is about building credibility and trust between the two parties. It is a step in building a meaningful partnership.

You have undoubtedly heard the phrase "win-win," popularized by Stephen Covey in his best-selling book *The 7 Habits of Highly Effective People*. Simply put, it means that in order to achieve a win for one's self, we must allow the other person to win also. Sounds altruistic, but is the concept practical? We know that in sports, if one side wins, the other side must have lost. In a courtroom, likewise, one side wins and the other loses.

Instead, we like to use the phrase "gain-gain." No one has to "win" at another's expense. Rather, if both sides of a situation gain, everyone benefits.

How do we get to gain-gain? Through engaging stakeholders in meaningful dialogue and sharing knowledge, both sides gain. Knowledge is power, so we are ultimately sharing power. That, in turn, builds the satisfaction levels of our stakeholders, builds our credibility with them, and increases the trust between us.

What would the power of gain-gain have meant in the plant-expansion scenario we discussed earlier? If company management had gone to their community, engaged in dialogue with their neighbors, and shared information about their expansion plans, they could have addressed concerns from the public before the ill-fated public hearing.

Perhaps the neighbors were concerned about increased truck traffic in and out of the plant because of the expansion. If the company knew that the additional number of trucks would be minimal, they could share that, thus allaying neighbors' fears. If the concern was about having trucks on the highway near the plant while school buses were traveling the same route, you could find a compromise wherein the trucks would be limited during those times. In either of these outcomes, the concept of gain-gain applies. Your credibility is heightened and trust increased.

The end result is that you get your permit, the neighbors have their concerns dealt with, and a bridge has been built for stronger future relationships.

Gain-gain leads to success for all involved. For industry, it means they gain the opportunity to move forward with their initiatives. For the neighbors, it means they gain the opportunity to contribute to the dialogue. For everyone, it leads to sustained environments, communities, and jobs.

Chapter One *True Spin* Takeaways

- Feelings of lack of control lead the public to frustration, anger, and mistrust.

- Feelings of satisfaction have a direct correlation with how much control one has in a given situation.

- Listen to people to build credibility with them.

- Build credibility to build trust.

- Work toward gain-gain opportunities by sharing power.

- Gain-gain opportunities lead to success.

CHAPTER TWO

A Little History

A quiet revolution has taken place in communities throughout the United States. Citizens are regularly telling local industry what they think of them as neighbors. Plant managers are asking their neighbors how they feel about future facility plans. Relationships are being built, one meeting at a time. Trust is blossoming in unlikely partnerships.

This hasn't always been the case. In her 1962 book *Silent Spring*, Rachel Carson declared, "For the first time in the history of the world, every human being is now subjected to contact with dangerous chemicals, from the moment of conception until death." Carson's book arguably signaled the start of the environmental movement.

Nevertheless, it wasn't until the 1970s that business became concerned—or interested—in what environmental activists had to say. Industry believed they had the right to run their operations without interference from the public. And, for the most part, their neighbors were content to have the good-paying jobs and accept the pollution as the "smell of money."

Many industry leaders started from a "none of your business" mentality, believing that neighbors had no right to information about their operations, that the facts about operations were proprietary, and that managers didn't have time to spend on communicating. That was about to change.

The tragic accident in Bhopal, India, in 1984 altered the landscape forever. Citizens living near chemical plants became scared. They demanded to know more about what was happening behind those gray corporate walls. Elected officials responded to public concerns. Laws were passed to protect citizens from potential dangers and put information about plant operations in the hands of the public for the first time.

After the Bhopal tragedy, lesser but well-publicized incidents in the United States created fears among those who lived near chemical plants. Activist groups were formed, and national environmental groups took up the cause. The outcry led elected officials on the local and national levels to propose and enact regulations to address concerns. As a result, industry leaders began to realize the importance of sharing information about their operations. They thought that by educating the local citizenry, the volume of concern would be lowered.

To some extent, this strategy worked. Local residents were surprised to hear from managers, and in some cases the information was enough to tamp down the voices of opposition. But this approach didn't get to the heart of the problem. Doling out information is a one-way street. Listening is something else, and few were listening to their neighbors' anxieties about living next to a facility they believed could cause them harm.

Enter the US Congress. I attended many of the hearings held at then West Virginia State College (now University) in Institute, West Virginia, next to the sprawling chemical complex housing the sister unit to the one in Bhopal. In these hearings, members of Congress listened as concerned citizens, anxious emergency responders, and local elected officials expressed fear and frustration about what they didn't know about chemical plants. People, many of whom I had known for over a decade, passionately demanded to know what chemicals in the plants could harm them. They wanted to know what was being done to protect them. They wanted a say in how operations were managed. All of us who attended the hearings knew things were going to change.

Legislation came swiftly, despite the opposition of some industry groups and others decrying the intrusion of government into private business operations. People felt they had the right to know what was in these facilities, and Congress agreed. They passed the Emergency Planning and Community Right-to-Know Act (EPCRA) in 1986.

EPCRA's primary purpose is to inform communities and citizens of chemical hazards in their area. It requires state environmental agencies to annually collect data on releases and transfers of certain toxic chemicals from industrial facilities and make the data available to the public. The US Environmental Protection Agency (USEPA) maintains this information in a database called the Toxic Release Inventory (TRI).

EPCRA also includes provisions requiring state and local governments to do more to plan for the possibility of accidents. This prompted many communities with industrial complexes to develop full-scale emergency plans with the industry and to install community notification sirens and telephone alert systems.

Spurred by activist groups and concerned citizens, Congress moved further to assure that citizens knew the risks of living near a chemical plant by encouraging the USEPA to do more to help inform and educate citizens about these risks. In 1993, the USEPA developed a draft of a sweeping regulation that would require facilities that use or store certain types of regulated materials to provide information about the substances to local emergency responders, elected officials, and the public. The regulation had the provocative provision that became known as the "worst-case scenario" provision—

plants would be required to tell their communities what was the worst possible accident that could occur and how many people could be harmed.

Because it was so uniquely qualified for the task, the agency asked the Kanawha Valley in West Virginia—known as the "chemical valley"—to conduct a test run. It was the perfect location to run such a test. The Kanawha Valley was the birthplace of the petrochemical industry and had a long history of providing good jobs that were the bedrock of a strong economy.

To their credit, industry in and around Charleston, West Virginia, in the Kanawha Valley banded together and created "Safety Street." Each local plant developed informational materials describing the chemicals they stored in significant quantities. Using computer models, they created plume maps depicting the "kill zones" for the worst possible accident. Some of the maps were downright frightening—showing kill zones covering a sixty-mile radius from the source of the accident. Historical information about significant accidents was also included.

The plants also provided citizens with information about all the efforts they take to prevent such an accident from occurring and described how they would respond should an accident occur.

Many of our industrial clients were involved in the effort, and we helped them create displays in the local mall, develop handouts, and prepare spokespersons to address the media and public about the detailed information never before shared with the public. We encouraged the plants with whom we worked to engage with their neighbors in separate meetings to have more dialogue about the information.

Perhaps to the amazement of industry, the public's response was mostly positive. Media covered the story with the appropriate perspective that the kill zones were unrealistic. Emergency responders applauded the effort as a move toward better preparedness. It was a good first step toward transparency.

In June 1996, the USEPA issued the final regulation. The rule, formally named the Risk Management Plan, followed closely the draft used in Safety Street. It would be the first time that such information as worst-case scenarios would be widely shared with the public. Based on the practices in the West Virginia test, the rule also called for information on ways the plant worked to eliminate or reduce hazards, prevent incidents, minimize or contain incidents, respond promptly to emergencies, and prepare the public for possible incidents.

Perhaps the most important aspect of this legislation was that industry and citizens were openly talking and listening to one another, arguably for the first time.

After the terrorist attacks on 9/11, the legislation was modified to prevent would-be terrorists from gaining access to information that would allow them to target industrial facilities storing hazardous materials. Some companies chose to retreat from sharing information with the public, perhaps using 9/11 as an excuse to withdraw from community engagement, potentially breaking the trust that had formed.

While some industry leaders labeled much of the legislation a burden on industry, good things have come about as a result. Companies are proactively talking with their neighbors and local activists. They recognize the value of a dialogue with these groups. And they are beginning to build credibility and, ultimately, trust with their neighbors.

As we discussed in chapter 1, these dialogues fill a basic human need for the neighbors. We all want to be in control of our lives—of what is going on around us and what is happening to us.

Chapter Two *True Spin* Takeaways

∴ Industry has moved from isolationism to "educating" the public about their operations, to listening to their concerns, to engaging them in meaningful dialogue.

∴ Legislation has formalized, and in some cases spurred, dialogue between industry and communities.

∴ More and more, industry is recognizing the value of public engagement.

CHAPTER THREE

Public Participation in the Regulated Industries

The public has a great deal of power if they choose to use it. Regulations like the ones we discussed in the previous chapter ensure that citizens have a large amount of information about industrial operations. They are given tons of data from state and federal regulators regarding the safety and environmental performance of most heavy industries.

Virtually every major permitting process requires public involvement. Built into the permit schedule is time for the public to view the proposed permit and provide feedback to the regulatory agency. Often a public hearing will be held where people who are interested in the permit can come to voice their support or concern. Sometimes, with complex issues, a public information session may be part of the process. These all serve to help local interested citizens have a voice in how the permit is finally written and sometimes in determining whether the permit is issued or not.

But sometimes the regulator's formal process isn't enough. In reality, many of these forums are less than productive. They are designed to get public input but not establish a dialogue. Citizens can make statements, but often their questions remain unanswered. Most companies are either not invited to explain their operations or choose not to do so in a setting that doesn't allow for give and take. Media coverage of these events can lead activists to use the hearing as a public relations tool against the company. In reality, public hearings rarely address real issues and almost never serve the company's or the public's best interests.

The public hearing is dictated by the regulator and often is part of the prescribed regulatory process. That doesn't mean it has to be the only way a company communicates during a permitting process. In fact, it is the least effective way to gain public understanding and trust for industrial operations.

We've discussed before how trust is a critical element in developing sound relationships with your stakeholders, and we said having credibility is the door to building that trust. Public engagement is the key, then, to becoming a credible source of information for your community, workforce, and other stakeholders.

Here are a couple of examples of how public engagement helped a company achieve their goals while allowing the public a chance to share in the process.

Arch Coal wanted to take advantage of significant coal reserves and permit the construction and operation of an underground mine and preparation plant in the heart of West Virginia's southern coal fields. Historically, this area was highly unionized; in fact, the coal wars of the 1920s were held within a few miles of the new mine site. Also, environmentalists had been very active in the area against both surface and underground mining.

In a first for the coal industry, Ann Green Communications was asked to organize and facilitate a community advisory panel (CAP) as part of the company's efforts to construct and operate the mine. Company officials announced the formation of the CAP at the public event publicizing the opening of the mine. The CAP would serve as a forum for concerned neighbors to discuss all aspects of the mine's development and operation.

A cross section of interested neighbors was selected to participate on the CAP, and the panel was seated before ground was broken on the new mine. Members learned of every aspect of the project, including efforts to protect the environment, hiring practices, and transportation of coal from the mine. Roads and railroad tracks had to be moved. Homes were purchased to make way for the mine. All these challenges were discussed openly at the CAP meetings. Problems were brought to the group and solutions were sought together.

This is a community located in an economically disadvantaged area. The coal industry is, or has been, responsible for the livelihoods of many of the residents. The CAP has given these families a forum to work together to protect and preserve an industry important to their county's heritage and economic sustainability while responding to community needs.

Folks in rural areas of Appalachia—and, indeed, across this land—share the values of faith, hard work, and love of family and country. In this particular community, the people are amazing. They have worked so hard all their lives. They take care of one another without a second thought. They are warm and welcoming, and it's easy to form lifelong friendships.

Of particular concern was maintaining local water quality. Because of the mine's water needs, Arch Coal persuaded the area water company to extend service to the area, not only for the mine but for the benefit of the community as well.

An old bridge still used by school buses was deemed unsafe for heavy coal trucks. The company built another bridge beside the old bridge and turned it over to the state for use by the public.

The residents in this community are very proud of the natural assets that surround them. CAP members, working side by side with mine personnel, have conducted roadside and river cleanup projects for the past several years. They applied for and received a Stream Partners grant for constructing a river access point and planting stabilizing vegetation on the river bank. The mine assisted in building a picnic area as well.

The CAP and mine personnel have worked cooperatively to revitalize Rockhouse Lake, a fourteen-acre pond reclaimed from an old mining property. The lake project began as a CAP initiative to clean up an underutilized recreational asset in the community. Over the past five years, it has evolved into a community development project, with partners ranging from local government agencies to local businesses and community organizations. The project now includes stocking the lake with bass and trout and building a handicap accessible pier. A pavilion and sports venues have been added. Through a grant from the local water company, the group was able to erect educational signs around the lake to help educate young people about the flora and fauna around the lake.

The CAP has been the focal point for many of the community's issues and neighbors' concerns. Because problems have been solved in the monthly meetings, lawsuits—so prevalent in projects like these—have been avoided. The community has benefited from access to safe public water supplies, a new and safer bridge, and the support of the mine for important community initiatives.

The mine, in turn, has benefited from tremendous support over the years. CAP members Diann Kish and Linda

Dials spearheaded efforts to enlist their friends, family, and neighbors for rallies in support of the mine's permitting needs and the coal industry in general. Diann is a lifelong resident of the area, a woman of great faith and happy spirit despite an often challenging life. Linda came to the area from Ohio, married a coal miner, and is raising her family here. She's a tireless worker for her family and community. They spoke in public meetings on the capital steps in Charleston and were featured in a CNN story, speaking up about the value of the coal industry and in support of their way of life.

Even in these difficult times for the coal industry, the mine continues to support the community's initiatives, including a safe Halloween party that provides a safe venue for about two hundred children annually. And the community continues to support the industry.

Changing Minds through Engagement

The next example comes from the cement industry and illustrates how public engagement can influence the decisions of regulators.

A quarry and cement plant located in Maryland had unsuccessfully tried to convince regulators to allow them to burn hazardous waste as an alternative fuel source in their kiln. Public opposition was spearheaded by an activist group of near neighbors who were particularly vocal in their condemnation of the idea. The plant's reputation was damaged, and ill feelings were prevalent.

I worked with the company and community to improve the frayed relationships in anticipation of the introduction of alternative fuel sources. Our first step was to establish a public participation process in the form of a CAP. Members of the panel included some of the very neighbors opposed to the plant's burning of hazardous waste. Although some of the initial meetings were contentious and full of distrust on both sides, the process worked to bring out the issues and lead the members to resolution.

A big reason for the success was their plant manager. This gentleman had been manager for many years and knew the operations inside and out. He was well respected by the employees for his open and forthright approach to management, and he took this same approach with the community. People learned to value what he said, and his honesty made them trust him.

Within six months of formation, the panel had gained enough understanding and trust in the plant that members were supportive of the plant's burning tires and waste wood for fuel. Even those quite skeptical about the new fuels were convinced that the measures the plant would take to manage the process were significant enough to warrant their confidence. They withdrew their opposition. With no public opposition, the regulators felt comfortable issuing the necessary permits for the plant to move forward. Some of the same individuals who had been vocal activists against the plant before spoke publicly in favor of the plant's initiatives as a result of their participation on the panel. They showed their support publicly by cohosting an open house at the plant and sponsoring a website to share what they had learned with the rest of the community. They provided support and guidance as the plant worked toward expansion of its quarry.

In both these examples, engaging the public in dialogue made all the difference in the outcomes for the companies involved.

Public engagement, also called public participation, is a process by which you engage your "publics" in face-to-face discussions about your operations. The success of the public participation process is based on the philosophy that when neighbors, community activists, and elected officials have an opportunity to participate in the process and understand issues involved in addressing safety, environmental, and other issues of concern, they are more likely to view the information shared with them as credible.

We've all had experiences in which we felt a point of view was being "crammed down our throats." Whether by a politician, boss, or other authority figure, this approach rarely, if ever, results in a supportive audience. Allowing the audience—in this case your stakeholders—to participate by engaging in dialogue about an issue increases the chances of garnering their support exponentially.

Public participation also helps develop trust in the communicators sharing the information. When the communicator is willing to listen to other points of view or concerns from the audience, the audience members are much more likely to be confident in the communicator and his or her message.

Finally, public participation increases confidence in the industry or company engaging the public and helps the public see them as an asset to their community.

Chapter Three *True Spin* Takeaways

⁘ Regulatory permitting processes require public involvement.

⁘ Public hearings may not be highly valuable in improving the public's understanding.

⁘ Community support—or opposition—can impact regulatory decisions.

⁘ Public participation develops public trust and increases confidence in industry.

CHAPTER FOUR

Understanding Your Audiences

We saw in the preceding chapter how important it is for companies to understand the wants and needs of their audiences. The trust of the public is not easily earned, but through public engagement, success is achievable.

A major component of a good public participation process is bringing together the right group of stakeholders. It may feel more comfortable to talk to a group of business leaders who understand the need for your jobs, but often that is not the constituency with whom you most need to engage.

Near neighbors and businesses nestled next to a plant often have a very different perspective. Environmental activists may be seeking different information than the Chamber of Commerce membership. All these audiences have valid points of view.

On many occasions, we have observed company leaders who believe the only audience that matters is local elected officials. They spend their energies on reaching out to the mayor or city council members, assuming that these individuals will lead public opinion in support of their initiatives. Without a doubt, government relations efforts are an important part of community relation building, but the industries that place their efforts on local officials alone can come to a rude awakening. Local elected officials try to stay close to their constituencies and, therefore, respond more quickly than state and national elected officials to what the public feels about different issues. They are responsive to those who put them in office. They became leaders in their communities by listening to those who cast ballots for them. If the voting public is up in arms about an issue, they are not likely to push back for the benefit of industry. They also are not likely to be your champion in the face of stiff community opposition.

Case in point—a small chemical plant in Morrisville, Pennsylvania.

A major chemical manufacturer had just acquired another smaller company. The acquisition included a small plant that made chemicals for the electronics industry located in Morrisville, a pleasant town north of Philadelphia. Shortly after the acquisition, the plant experienced a gas explosion that damaged a building and sent material into the community. Luckily, no one was seriously injured.

Prior to the incident, the local plant manager had been working to build relationships with elected officials but had not reached out to near neighbors. In this case, the phrase "near neighbors" was literal. The closest neighbor was across a two-lane street.

After the explosion, the community became outraged about the heretofore unknown danger in their midst. The outrage was so strong that the borough council initiated a resolution to have the plant closed.

The company's initial reaction was first to try to work with the few council members who were open to talking with them. Some members on the council refused to even meet with company representatives. With the resolution to close the plant looming over their heads, they changed course and decided to engage the public directly.

Ann Green Communications was asked to develop a way to involve the broad community in the discussion. We invited a cross section of residents, including many of their nearest neighbors, to attend a meeting. We asked the borough council if the meeting could be held in the council chambers, and the meeting was broadcast over the borough's cable television station. The chamber was filled with many angry citizens, but as facilitators, we were able to keep an orderly and process-driven session.

As experienced and knowledgeable facilitators, we add real value to the process. We organize the meetings and the discussions for maximum productivity, incorporating numerous opportunities for comments and questions. Using discussion leader techniques, we are able to draw out all ideas and encourage individual participation. We guide participants in brainstorming options for gain-gain, and we use weighted voting and problem-solving skills to assist the group and help them move forward. Ultimately, our goal is to help the company and group reach consensus.

Part of the process of helping in the Morrisville situation was to start the meeting by listening to community concerns, boarding them on easels, and promising to address those concerns during the meeting. In other words, the company listened first. Then they responded. Company representatives prepared diligently to convey what had happened and the steps they were taking to prevent a recurrence. As a result, they were able to illustrate the company's commitment to improving safety and protecting the community.

Subsequent meetings built on the positive first meeting. Additional key opinion leaders, including borough council members, were identified and brought into the discussions. After several months of open and candid discussions, the council withdrew the plant closure resolution because the community furor over the incident had subsided substantially.

A key ingredient in this company's success was the correct identification of stakeholders to participate in their community meetings. Recognizing who in the community were leaders of public opinion was critical. Before bringing the final group together, we interviewed many people and held focus groups with plant employees who were from the local area. Research made all the difference.

While this story has a positive ending, it illustrates the challenges that can occur when you have to forge new relationships in the midst of a crisis. The plant had to build bridges to a new community while responding to the crisis.

Community Factions

All communities are made up of many factions, but there are specific groups into which most citizens will fall. Originally identified by Dr. Peter Sandman, recognized as the father of risk communications, we've evolved our own take on the list.

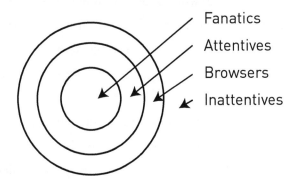

STAKEHOLDERS

Fanatics
Attentives
Browsers
Inattentives

We call the factions Fanatics, Attentives, Browsers, and Inattentives—all distinct groups of citizens requiring varying degrees of engagement. The circles represent the relative size of the different factions, with the Inattentives being the remaining universe of people beyond the other three levels.

Fanatics, as the word suggests, are highly interested in the issue at hand and have strongly held beliefs or viewpoints. In the extreme, Fanatics might include those who would march in protest over an issue or use civil disobedience to oppose something. It is unlikely that they will change their point of view, and they are constantly trying to move others to see their perspective.

Attentives are interested citizens who like to be informed and are willing to do some homework to gain that knowledge. They will attend meetings, research topics on the Internet, and reach out to elected officials for answers or to share their thoughts. This group, in fact, would likely include elected officials.

Browsers are generally interested in what is going on around them and will make a minimal effort to remain informed of current events. They are unlikely, however, to leave their homes to attend meetings about a topic. They generally get their knowledge through the Internet or traditional media.

Inattentives are folks who are generally not interested in current events beyond what affects them directly. They include people whose lives are too busy or burdened to engage in anything beyond what is required.

On any given issue, any of us might fall into a different category. For example, a person might not be the least bit interested in the new industrial facility being built up the road but will be a Fanatic about a problem at the high school where their children attend.

None of these categories of citizens is greater or lesser than the others. We all will fall into all of them at one time or another. If you are trying to engage a community in public participation, the trick is to know your audience and select mostly Attentives to engage.

Attentives, as noted, will come to meetings, work to learn about an issue, and be willing to listen and share their ideas. They are ideal candidates for community advisory panels (CAPs) and similar engagement groups.

Browsers are not reliable as group members and are happy to learn about a given issue through the media or Internet. Inattentives, by their nature, are uninterested. Neither group's general indifference is likely to change unless they are moved to become more attentive by some outside force. For example, if a Browser hears information about the industrial facility that makes them feel it could cause them or their family harm, they might quickly move to Attentive. The same would be true of an Inattentive.

People also can move from Attentive to Browser or Inattentive. This movement usually comes from learning new information that makes them less interested in or concerned about a particular topic. In the case study noted at the beginning of this chapter, near neighbors of the plant that experienced the gas explosion moved from Fanatic to Attentive—even to Inattentive—the longer the company engaged with them. The more they learned about the plant's operation, the less concerned they became and the less they needed to remain engaged. Those who remained engaged did so because they felt it important for the plant managers and community to continue a dialogue about a variety of plant and community issues. They also felt the need to keep a check on the plant to be sure the plant management met their commitments to safety and to the environment. It was a "trust but verify" approach for some.

As we have said, trust is the goal in public interaction. What are the pathways to being trusted by each of our stakeholder groups?

Each group will want and need different information. Fanatics may never agree with your point of view but deserve to be heard and to receive factual information from you. Remember that the other groups of stakeholders will be observing how you interact with those who might disagree with your point of view. Treating Fanatics with respect and making every effort to respond to their questions is the appropriate approach. Becoming angry or refusing to talk with the Fanatics can cause Attentives to question your motives.

Attentives will seek out information from all points of view. Of all the stakeholder groups, they are the most important in terms of developing relationships. While it is common to become obsessed with dealing with the Fanatics, it is more important to listen to and satisfy the Attentives. Spend your time focusing on their needs, listening to them carefully, and responding to their inquiries factually.

Browsers will develop their opinions from resources that are easy to obtain. This audience will appreciate receiving a newsletter or viewing a posting online and will rely on media to gather their facts. As a result, you will want to be sure to meet the needs of local media and develop your own social media platform in order to reach this audience.

Just because Inattentives are not currently interested in whatever the issue may be doesn't mean they can't be awakened to the issue. By taking care of the other stakeholder groups, you will likely meet the needs of Inattentives, thus reducing the opportunity for them to become discontent.

We've now categorized the stakeholders so that we can better develop and target our messages to meet their needs and ours. Let's turn our attention to the process of building credibility and, ultimately, trust.

The first tenet of public participation is making a commitment to involving the public in the decisions you make that can affect them or their lifestyles. This doesn't mean you have to reveal your trade secrets or inner workings. What it does mean is that you provide information related to the public interest, you listen to their concerns about your operations, and you take into account their feedback when making decisions about those operations.

A simple example will illustrate this concept. A plant in Ohio was working to clean up an old manufacturing site. The cleanup process involved taking waste material from the site to a hazardous waste facility by truck. The removal plan had been blessed by regulators. The trucks to be used in the removal were newer, were in good condition, and were to be covered with tarps to prevent material from spilling on the roadway. The road from the plant to a major highway was a two-lane road shared with the public, but there were only going to be about ten new trucks coming and going during the day.

The public was immediately outraged by the plant's announcement to use trucks to remove the material from the site during the remediation process.

Initially, plant management was confused by the upheaval. We were invited to assist in identifying what the concerns were. We started by listening to their neighbors and involved them in the process. We quickly discovered the source of the discontent. The trucks were going to be running all day long, a departure from the normal truck traffic in and out of the plant. The heavy vehicles would be on the small road at the same time that school buses were picking up children in the morning and returning them home in the afternoon. With a simple adjustment in the trucking schedule, and a promise to avoid the bus delivery times, the problem was solved and everyone gained. We still work with the company and community to keep the lines of communication open.

Had the plant managers more fully involved their neighbors in the initial plans, the problem would have been solved before the public became angry. Consider people's feelings when making decisions. In this case, the fears of parents that their children might be hurt by a truck were real, and recognizing those fears earlier in the process would have prevented anxiety on both sides. Involvement of the public in decisions that affect their lives is paramount in building credibility and trust.

Honesty is another tenet of public participation. Give honest answers to questions from the public. If you don't know something, say you don't know. If you make a mistake, admit it. Correct the record whenever it should be set straight. Speak in terms people can understand. Avoid engineer-speak and industry jargon, which can be construed as a way to avoid providing straightforward information to the public. All of these are basic in building honest relationships with your stakeholders.

Finally, remember that you are human and so are your stakeholders. Show empathy when it is called for. Put yourself in the other's shoes when confrontation takes place. Share your personal life experiences when appropriate. If you are dealing with an upset parent, for example, relate as a parent yourself. Be prepared to respond to personal questions. You don't need to give out private information, but recognize that a personal question often is a sign that someone is trying to relate to you on a personal level.

One quick story illustrates how you can be too candid, however. An otherwise pleasant and thoughtful plant manager of a chemical plant in Kentucky once was asked by a plant neighbor why he and his family didn't live in the town where his plant was located. He paused for a moment, then said, "My wife didn't think the homes here were good enough." Yikes! Remember, every man's home is his castle, and every hometown is precious to the residents. Without realizing it, the plant manager insulted all his neighbors with one quick comment.

We discussed Fanatics as a stakeholder group that may include some near neighbors and local citizen activist groups. Other Fanatics may be professional, paid activists. Citizen activists are truly concerned and passionate advocates for their communities and point of view. Paid activists also have a passion for their cause and may be no less committed to it than citizen activists. The difference is that they also must work for support in order to be paid for what they do. Therefore, part of their effort usually involves fund raising. That can take the form of solicitation of members to a group where dues are paid. The professional activists also recognize that in order to perpetuate their organization, they must have a specific cause that rallies people to support their work, and they may target a specific company or plant as a result.

Professional activists serve an important role in the development of opposition groups. They organize Fanatics and other dedicated individuals to express their point of view effectively to the larger society. They often bring needed resources to a side of an issue that may not have those resources available to them.

Because their goals go beyond simply advocating for a position and they must also raise funds and promote their group, interacting with professional activists requires a different approach than that for other stakeholders.

First, it is important for industry to understand the goals of professional activist groups. Some activist groups are local or regional; others have a national presence. This can affect how they prefer to interact with industry—if they choose to interact with industry at all. Local professional activists are more vested in building their coalition than creating large coffers. National groups tend to be more active in lobbying Congress, building large coalitions, participating in media outreach, and building membership, which all take a lot of money and energy.

In both cases, it is important to engage the groups, understand their goals, share information about your side of the issue, and work with them for resolution. Particularly in the case of local and regional groups, identifying a goal that is mutually acceptable and meeting that goal can lead to a positive outcome for all involved—a gain-gain result.

A local environmental action group in Cincinnati, affiliated with the statewide organization Ohio Citizen Action, was contacted by residents in that city concerned about operations at a chemical plant, primarily because of unpleasant odors. The groups worked together to target the company. The local group recruited neighbors who lived near the plant to put signs in their yards along the truck route into the plant. They organized "bucket brigades" to capture air samples. Members of the brigade took special buckets around the neighborhood and captured air samples for analysis to see if the local plant was emitting harmful chemicals. They contacted local media to discuss their concerns about the odors. They petitioned the company's president and sent letters to its board of directors.

At first, the company's executives chose to ignore the protests, but after some time they realized that ignoring the protests was not an appropriate way to deal with the concerns. They hired us to engage the near neighbors and activists in a working group to discuss issues of concern. A working group is a smaller group of people established to resolve one topic or issue. Initial meetings were contentious, but because we had the knowledge of the subject matter and skill in managing contentious discussions, we were able to keep the process on track. Both sides threatened to abandon the effort early on, but with patience, we were able to keep both sides at the table. In a few months, they were able to agree on a set of goals acceptable to all involved. Within six months, the protest signs were down.

A major reason the working group approach worked was that it gave all involved a meaningful place at the table. It also allowed the activists to play a public role in helping the neighbors accomplish their goals.

In another example of positive interaction with an environmental activist group, a plant was being targeted because of concern about the use of chlorine at the site. The chlorine was delivered to the site in railcars that traveled through local neighborhoods. We facilitated a CAP for the plant. As we worked with the environmental group, again affiliated with Ohio Citizen Action, we were able to identify a specific goal they had—they wanted to have the plant build an enclosure around the area where chlorine was offloaded to protect local residents from exposure should a spill occur. The company was able to design an enclosure that protected the neighbors but also was safe for the workers and the environment. With this goal met, the leaders of Ohio Citizen Action achieved public recognition, which helped in their recruiting efforts, so they moved away from targeting this company. The company was able to continue operating with a better relationship with their near neighbors and improved safety measures. Everyone gained in the transaction.

These scenarios worked for these companies and these communities. No two communities are alike. Just as an engineer wouldn't build a plant without researching the best approach and developing a plan of action, neither should public engagement be done without the proper research and planning.

Know your stakeholders. We've discussed the categories of stakeholders, from Fanatics to Inattentives, and how important it is to engage the Attentives in your community. But how do you determine who they are? The answer: research.

Community leaders come from all walks of life. Elected officials are obvious stakeholders, but remember that they respond to the needs and concerns of the voting public first. Engaging the unofficial leaders is just as important. Identify leaders within your school system, ministerial association, and business and medical communities. Ask your employees who live in the community to tell you who they feel are leaders. Once you know your audience, the next step is identifying the best way to engage with them.

Chapter Four *True Spin* Takeaways

- ⁘ Local elected officials usually follow the desires of their electorate, not lead them.

- ⁘ Communities are made up of many kinds of stakeholders:

  - O Fanatics are highly interested in, and motivated by, an issue.

  - O Attentives are interested in an issue and will engage in dialogue about it.

  - O Browsers are somewhat interested but would rather get their information through media or other passive means.

  - O Inattentives are not interested in a particular issue and can be satisfied by satisfying the other stakeholders.

- ⁘ People can move from one classification of stakeholder to another.

- ⁘ Paid, professional activists have unique goals; industry is wise to understand these groups and engage with them.

CHAPTER FIVE

Embracing the Public Participation Process

A form of surface mining, known as "mountaintop removal," has become a very contentious environmental issue in key coal mining states, including West Virginia.

In early 1999, the West Virginia legislature passed Senate Bill 681, the "mountaintop removal bill," which called for the West Virginia Department of Environmental Protection (WVDEP) to create and establish rules for an "Office of Explosives and Blasting." Aware of the controversial nature of mountaintop removal and the bill itself, the WVDEP asked Ann Green Communications to create a stakeholder working group that would assist in developing the proposed rules and to facilitate the process. Approximately forty representatives from several stakeholder groups were invited to the organizational meeting. Stakeholder groups included citizens and environmental advocates, vendors, blasting engineers and technologists, coal miners, and mining industry leaders.

This group faced many challenges. The citizens and environmental advocates were extremely distrustful of the coal industry. Relations between the two sides historically had been contentious, and this issue was particularly divisive. Over the years, activists had sometimes marched through the streets of coal communities, resulting in ugly shouting matches and worse. Placards for and against coal companies periodically dotted the landscape. And occasionally, fists flew. The coal industry usually worked to achieve its goals through government relations, and the idea of direct public engagement was foreign to them. Complicating matters, a coalition of environmental groups—including some of those at the stakeholders' table—was actively involved in a lawsuit against the WVDEP and mining companies to stop mountaintop removal.

The stakeholder group defined as its purpose: "To draft an effective blasting rule with the consensus of all affected parties." We led the group in creating a team agreement, reviewed at every meeting, which committed the participants to treat one another with respect and to stay on task.

The process limited discussion to provisions of the WVDEP's proposed rules within the confines of the enabling legislation. Otherwise, the various participating factions would have tried to debate their feelings about mountaintop removal, derailing the process. Strict adherence to this goal was essential to the completion of the project.

Each and every stakeholder had the opportunity to offer amendments, additions, or deletions to the draft legislation. These were then discussed in an effort to reach consensus. Consensus was defined as a state in which participants either positively supported the provision or could consent to it as the best possible alternative in the circumstances. In order for a portion of the rule to be marked as having been approved "by consensus," there could be no objection. It was the intent of this process to provide every stakeholder an equal voice.

Despite assurance that each opinion would be given equal weight, citizen and environmental advocate stakeholders stated in the initial meeting that they felt outnumbered by representatives of other stakeholder groups, who they believed generally supported mountaintop removal and, therefore, opposed their position. In an attempt to ease this concern, citizen and environmental advocate stakeholders were given more seats at the table than any other single stakeholder group. This was achieved with the consensus of all stakeholders in the initial meeting. Citizen/advocate stakeholders also stated for the record their belief that this particular bill failed to adequately address their concerns over mountaintop removal. Some found it frustrating to have discussion limited to the proposed rule.

The vast majority of time spent discussing the WVDEP's proposed rules was enormously constructive. Stakeholders representing all sides engaged in positive, practical dialogue, and minutes of the meetings were posted on the Internet each week for the public to review. Most stakeholders left the contentious nature of the battle over mountaintop removal outside the meeting room. Each week, these individuals brought their own unique perspectives and experience to discussion of a complex subject while maintaining a vision of the ultimate goal, which was to create rules that would best serve the interests of the people of West Virginia. The project was completed on time. The group's final report passed through public comment, and the proposed legislation was adopted by the West Virginia legislature.

This is an excellent example of the public participation process at work. Key stakeholders were identified and brought together in one room, and then they worked to identify a common goal, engaging in open and honest dialogue to meet that goal.

Good public participation programs share common threads. Citizens must be provided information about industrial activities in their communities, not just as a result of right-to-know laws but also under social sustainability tenets. When concerned stakeholders have an opportunity to participate in the process and understand issues involved in addressing safety, environmental, and other issues of concern, they are more likely to view the information shared with them as credible, develop trust in the communicators, and have confidence the industry will be an asset to their community. Even in this age of social media, nothing replaces human interaction when dealing with challenging topics. Public participation works because it allows communities to see industry not as a gray corporate wall but as earnest individuals trying to do a job. Those jobs often include developing products, or ingredients for products, that the public wants and needs. Making the connection about what is being made in an industrial facility and how that product goes into other products that fulfill consumer needs is a major goal of public participation. When people understand that the alphabet-soup chemical made at the local plant goes into their toothpaste or car seat or needed medicine, they have a logical reason why the chemical needs to be produced. Similarly, when the surface mining operation down the road extracts materials needed to make fertilizer to feed the world, the mining practice makes more sense. While corporations must make a profit to remain in business, they also must make products that meet human needs to be profitable. This fact sometimes gets lost.

The American Chemical Council (ACC), within their Responsible Care® program, has long established the value of interacting with the people who live near chemical manufacturing facilities. Developing and maintaining an ongoing dialogue is a cornerstone of the CAER (Community Awareness and Emergency Response) Code of Responsible

Care®. I have written guidance manuals for ACC on establishing community advisory panels (CAPs). It is through this ongoing and earnest interaction that companies earn the privilege to operate and help sustain the communities in which they operate. Without this privilege, companies can be shut down by a public that feels ignored and mistreated.

The USEPA encourages, and occasionally has mandated, the use of small community groups to provide ongoing input to a plant or at a Superfund or other remediation project that has the potential to affect the public.

There are, however, cautionary notes. Do not engage the public to serve only your own purposes. For a public participation program to be successful, all sides must gain from the experience. Do not establish a community dialogue to check off a box. Go into public participation with a desire to engage the public and work toward mutually beneficial goals and solutions. If you take the "check off the box" approach, it is a waste of both your time and resources and is likely to result in worse relationships with your public.

Case in point: A now-defunct coal company in southern West Virginia was strongly encouraged by the WVDEP to establish a dialogue with the citizens of a small town where they operated. Community residents had been expressing frustration with the regulators because the coal company had not been responsive to their concerns about the coal dust collecting on their homes as a result of coal trucks moving through the town.

Reluctantly, the company started meeting with local citizens. We were hired to facilitate the process. The company found it easy to make promises when confronted by upset neighbors in open meetings. One commitment was for the mine to purchase a street sweeper to clean the town's streets on a regular basis. The mine president was supportive of the compromise. But when the CEO of the parent company was informed of the idea, he brazenly said he didn't owe the citizens that courtesy and refused to allow the mine to keep its commitment. The promise appeared to be just a stall tactic, and as a result the citizens were more upset than before dialogue was initiated. Ultimately, the mine was forced to spend a considerable amount of money to install pollution control equipment. Failing to keep a promise cost this company in resources and public opinion.

Another pitfall is expecting results in an unreasonably short time. Solid relationships usually aren't formed overnight. Have realistic expectations. Allow enough time before expecting too much support from members of the public. Build credibility—then seek their trust.

Industrial facilities that are geographically close to similar facilities may find value in collaborating to create an ongoing dialogue with their common community. Just be sure your goals are the same or similar. If one manager feels the public participation initiative should be undertaken solely for the benefit of the companies while others recognize the value of a mutually beneficial arrangement, the collaboration won't work.

Use a third-party negotiator/facilitator to help with the process. An independent facilitator provides a buffer between the facility and an angry neighborhood. Using an independent facilitator adds an element of credibility to the process because the neutral negotiator serves to make sure all parties are heard. Be sure to engage one who is well versed in environmental, health, and safety issues directly related to your industry.

The most common form of public engagement for several years, particularly in the chemical industry, has been the CAP. Hundreds of these groups exist throughout the country and serve a variety of industries. Why are companies investing their time and resources in CAPs? Why do CAPs work? Why do they build trust?

A CAP is a group of usually about twenty individuals who represent the fabric of their community. They meet with plant managers regularly to discuss issues of mutual interest. Companies share their plans for the future and how they are meeting any safety and environmental challenges. Neighbors express what worries them about living near the facility and provide advice to the plant in response to community concerns.

A CAP is not a public relations program designed to improve the image of a facility or industry. Nor is it an activist group for the purpose of closing down a local plant. It is not a surrogate for the plant's spokesperson, either.

Most CAPs have been well received by both communities and industry. Most continue for many years, and only a few have stopped meeting altogether. Plant managers are learning how important engaging in dialogue with their neighbors can be. Communities are surprised at the openness of the managers about their operations, their challenges, and their future plans. Some really important issues are being addressed at the meetings. Some special friendships are being forged.

A CAP should be a forum for open and honest dialogue between citizens and plants to break down stereotypes and "corporate walls." Ultimately, a CAP provides the opportunity for building mutual respect and trust.

To best represent the fabric of the community, a CAP's membership must be broad based. Those responsible for its development must make every effort to involve all their key audiences within the community. These audiences—or stakeholders—may include environmental groups, civic leaders, business leaders, homemakers, hourly workers, and individuals who represent key elements of a community such as clergy, health care providers, emergency responders, and educators. Special attention should be given to ensure that the panel reflects the diversity within the community, including minority groups.

Unfortunately, not all CAPs are highly functioning. In too many, meetings are monologues from the site manager to a dwindling number of members willing to listen. Membership isn't as broad based as it needs to be. Plant managers are reluctant to have detractors participate along with supporters, thus improperly validating their own assumptions about the community. Long-term viability is questionable because they aren't focusing on the community's needs alongside those of the plant.

However, examples of successful CAPs are many. We will share several examples throughout this book where CAPs have been an integral part of the public engagement program and even a valuable part of a crisis response scenario. Many CAP members have shown a willingness to help companies and their communities in tangible ways.

Each CAP is unique, but they share common threads. Most CAPs want to discuss health, safety, and environmental issues with the sponsoring company or companies. Panel members are often interested in learning about the local, state, and federal regulations that govern the facility. Often they are interested in learning about local and corporate policies, such as those regarding purchasing from local vendors versus through corporate contracts and hiring locally.

In some cases, the plant's history in the community is important to the members. Perhaps there has been a history of accidents or labor disputes. Misinformation may be prevalent in the community, and the CAP will give you the opportunity to clarify your plant's past actions.

CAP members are often eager to know what is in store for your facility in the future. Will you be expanding, or are you planning a downturn or closure? You may not be able to answer all their questions, but understanding their interest allows you to be prepared to respond with as much information as is feasible.

If your operations involve chemicals or other sources of potential odors, you can expect CAP members to want to understand the origin of the odors and whether they pose any health risks. Members may ask whether they should contact the plant if they notice unpleasant odors. At the urging of panel members, some of our clients have chosen to establish an odor notification telephone line. In other situations, CAP members have been asked to inform the plant if unpleasant odors are noticeable in the community—a sort of "odor patrol." Citizens have the right to contact the regulatory agencies when they smell offensive odors, but isn't it better if they have enough of a relationship with the offending plant to contact them directly to seek resolution?

Traffic, both truck and train, can be an issue of interest. This is particularly true if trains block roadways on a regular basis or if truck traffic increases significantly. In chapter 4, we discussed how one plant solved a community concern over increased truck traffic by working out a schedule that eliminated trucks traveling a two-lane road when school buses were scheduled to pick up and deliver children—a great example of gain-gain.

Where plants could pose a safety risk to a community, it is very common for CAPs to learn about measures the plant takes to prevent accidents from occurring, such as process safety management measures. Panel members will be interested in understanding what the plant will do if an incident occurs, particularly one that has the potential of impacting the community. Adding the local emergency responders, including fire and police departments and members of the Local Emergency Planning Committee (LEPC), on the CAP is recommended for this reason.

For chemical plants, sharing data from your Toxics Release Inventory (TRI) report on an annual basis is recommended. This helps the community understand the history of emissions from your plant, which for the vast majority of plants in the United States is a trend line that has gone down every year since the reports were first released to the public. Reviewing your TRI report also gives you the opportunity to discuss ways you work to reduce emissions.

Chemical plants also should plan to discuss your Risk Management Plans if your operations fall under this regulation. The risks you pose, what you do to prevent them, and the ways you can mitigate any issues that do occur are all important to share with your CAP.

CAPs are often interested in activities that assist education and other civic needs in their area. Many of our groups work with their sponsoring plants to provide mini-grants to their local schools. Mini-grants are monetary sums, usually $100 to $500, awarded to primary or secondary school classes. They are designed to aid school classes in studying a specific science or environmental problem and may be used for developing study materials or displays, taking field trips, or purchasing equipment. Usually, CAP members administer the grant program and select the recipients, making it an easy way for the plant to support local education with minimal effort. This program is an excellent example of how a CAP can add value to your operations.

Producing a resource manual for educators is another worthwhile project. A resource manual can provide educators with a guide to programs that may benefit their students, offering a summary of available educational resources provided by area corporations. This is particularly effective for multi-company CAPs.

Another option, a "Science and Industry Day," is based on the traditional science fair, with the CAP serving as the host organization. Student science projects are displayed throughout the day, and keynote speakers and demonstrations by area industry are also featured. (If you have a mini-grant program, the classes can display what they have accomplished with their grant.) The event provides an opportunity for students to showcase their knowledge of science and the environment, while area residents can see how industry is involved in their community.

In some locations, special training programs for teachers are available and can be administered through the CAP. The purpose of these programs is to promote interest in chemistry and chemistry-related careers by building teacher leaders, developing partnerships, and providing hands-on experiments. Again, the CAP can serve as the initiating group. One important benefit of these programs is that they give teachers a better understanding of and appreciation for industry. Teachers have such an influence on young minds, and if they understand the value of the industry in their town they can encourage youngsters to explore industrial career opportunities down the road.

One unique opportunity a CAP can provide is a "Good Neighbor Night," an open meeting attended by CAP members, industry representatives, and community members who wish to find out more about the CAP and their sponsoring companies. A Good Neighbor Night is designed to create dialogue between area residents and local industries outside of CAP meetings.

Partnering with a CAP is also an excellent way for a plant to accomplish the task of training the community on how to shelter in place, educating local residents on what to do to ensure their safety in the event of an emergency. CAP members can be trained to give basic presentations about sheltering in place to local schools and civic and other organizations, which can take some of this burden from plant personnel.

Two other programs common to CAPs are highway cleanups and household hazardous waste collections. Highway cleanups allow CAP members an opportunity to get together outside of the regular CAP meetings and participate as a group in an activity that aids the environment. In a similar way, household hazardous waste collection efforts offer a chance for community members to help preserve the environment directly through their own efforts.

After CAPs have met with an industry for some time, members often wish to share what they are learning with a broader audience. In these instances, plants might choose to support the group in developing a newsletter or annual report to the community. These publications focus on what the CAP has discussed, information that all agree would be valuable to the greater community, and activities the panel has undertaken. It gives members a chance to share what they have learned, brings the information the company has provided the panel to a larger audience, and raises the greater community's awareness of the CAP. In recent years, CAPs and companies have opted for Facebook pages and websites to accomplish these goals.

As we have noted, CAPs are increasingly interested in communicating with the rest of the community about what they have learned—publishing newsletters or annual reports, sponsoring special outreach meetings, and speaking out as informed citizens in public meetings and hearings about issues important to the plants.

Highly functioning CAPs are sitting focus groups of mostly Attentives. The sponsoring industries can test their ideas and initiatives by vetting them through the CAP. The insight they receive from the CAP should mirror the opinions of the greater community.

CAPs allow plant managers to engage in real dialogue with their neighbors and other key stakeholders, with all working together to meet community needs and respond to industrial challenges.

A major value of a CAP to industrial managers is that it is a real time saver for managers, as it allows them to connect with the plant's core constituents in an organized and well-functioning setting at scheduled times. The meetings often eliminate the need for managers to have a number of individual meetings with stakeholders, including elected officials and emergency responders.

The CAP process also allows members of the community to share their concerns with plant management, and panelists have the opportunity to obtain answers to their questions about the facilities in their area. Plant management is encouraged to be more accessible to the public through the CAP. Panel members can work with facility management to make meaningful changes in the way the plant communicates with the community at large regarding emergencies, plant expansions, or other operational issues.

Through participation in a CAP, plant managers can show their commitment to the community face-to-face. Panels also allow managers to learn more about community concerns and interests.

Once real dialogue is established, the CAP members become informed citizens about the industrial operations. As they go about their lives, in their various work and home environments, they can share what they have learned in the meetings and be "experts" about the industry to their families, neighbors, and coworkers. In some instances, CAP members choose to provide support for the facility's initiatives.

The Mosaic Company, a phosphate mining company with operations in Florida, has embraced the CAP concept and has created a number of CAPs throughout their operating area. I'm pleased to facilitate one such group, located in

Manatee County. This is a terrific group of citizens with a broad range of interests. They include environmental activists and regulators, farmers, teachers, technical consultants, and emergency responders, as well as residents from many other walks of life—bright and interesting people all. Although we have been meeting together for over ten years, we always find more topics of interest every year than we have time to get to.

One year, we took on a particularly interesting and unique challenge. The CAP members asked to learn more about the arduous permitting process Mosaic must go through to initiate a new mining operation. CAP members studied the permitting process and, in conjunction with company representatives, decided to conduct a mock public meeting about a permit that Mosaic was seeking to expand mining operations in the area. The members role-played as company presenters, citizen advocates, and regulators. They worked hard to present a realistic hearing and then graded each other on how it was executed.

Through this exercise, the CAP members became fully familiar with the permitting process, and the company representatives were able to get invaluable feedback about the presentations they were to make before the real regulators. Mosaic became more aware of potential community concerns and was able to address those concerns in their presentation.

After going through the mock experience, several CAP members went to the actual public hearing and spoke in favor of Mosaic's plans. They were not asked to do so but chose to support the company after a full and open discussion of the pros and cons. They recognized the value that Mosaic brings to the community and the importance of the material they mine in feeding the world. Going through this experience helped solidify lasting relationships that continue today.

Public Engagement beyond CAPs

Public engagement is certainly not confined to plant sites, as we proved in our work for the American Petroleum Institute (API) a few years ago. API wanted to gain more knowledge about public attitudes toward the petroleum industry and to gauge public acceptability of API's initiatives. They asked Ann Green Communications to conduct a series of focus groups in various cities and towns throughout the United States.

Our task was to build upon existing public opinion surveys that had been conducted, to bore in on public attitudes and to test various potential initiatives. Working in focus group facilities from Seattle to Miami to San Diego to Providence, we met with carefully selected groups that included average citizens and those who identified themselves as environmental activists.

The participants were not blind, as they knew we were conducting the engagement exercises for API. Over the period of several months, we facilitated about twenty groups and gained a wealth of feedback about attitudes toward the petroleum industry. We were also able to "test" an outreach program that API was considering and give the organization valuable insight into how it would be received. As a result,

API was able to revise their program with full understanding of the public's response.

API, as a national trade organization, wasn't able to engage in the type of ongoing dialogue a CAP might provide, but through the focus groups we were able to tap into the sentiments of an array of opinions from across the nation. API was able to move forward with an understanding of what the public generally felt about their programs.

Chapter Five *True Spin* Takeaways

∴ ~~Good public participation programs share common~~ threads:

○ Citizens receive information about industry's issues and initiatives.

○ Human interactions break down "gray corporate walls."

○ For a public participation program to be successful, all sides must gain from the experience.

○ Don't engage the public just to "check off a box."

∴ Community advisory panels (CAPs) are a valuable tool in establishing stakeholder dialogue, but there are other valuable ways to achieve your goals.

CHAPTER SIX

Getting Permission to Operate

Industry must seek permission from a regulator or regulators to construct or operate a manufacturing plant. Today more than ever, that requirement includes seeking permission from the public. Without public acceptance, many potential projects are stopped before they ever get started.

Public participation is an important—often critical—part of the permitting process.

Ann Green Communications has used its public participation philosophy of open and honest dialogue to assist industry in reaching out to concerned and often distrustful citizens. The results have allowed the industry to gain understanding of its host community, to communicate key messages, to gain support for their plans, and ultimately to gain the permit needed to construct the facility. The following case studies further illustrate the concept of True Spin.

US WindForce desired a permit to construct and operate a wind generating facility in the northeastern portion of West Virginia. In an already sensitive area with regard to wind energy, the company faced potential opposition from environmentalists and concerned community leaders and residents. US WindForce realized the approach to securing the permit had to be dealt with differently than previous projects in the state and region.

Ann Green Communications created a communications plan to effectively convey information regarding the company's plans, the benefits to the community, and why the project was different from similar projects being planned and constructed in the region.

As we've said before, step one is to conduct research, in this instance to understand the community, local residents' needs, areas of interest, and opinions about wind energy. Our research helped us identify community leaders—both elected and opinion leaders—and determined that developing a community advisory panel (CAP) would benefit the project by bringing together these leaders and other key community representatives. The CAP could serve as a vehicle to introduce the company and provide a forum to identify both supporters and key activists.

We organized the CAP by selecting a cross section of community members and creating a forum through which communication would be managed. Company representatives shared information about every aspect of the project, including all studies required by the permitting process, efforts to protect the environment, and potential issues associated with wind energy, such as noise, flicker issues, and property values.

In addition to panel meetings, the company adopted a proactive style of outreach. We created a consistent stream of information to our target audiences via direct mail, handouts in local libraries, push emails, open houses, personal meetings with community and state leaders and elected officials, and presentations to local civic and governmental organizations. We used a hands-on approach with local, regional, and state media to position US WindForce as the key contact for project information. Positioning US WindForce as the expert on the topic limited dissemination of misinformation from others.

With input from the panel to shape the program, the company established a community benefit fund that provided needed financial resources for local organizations, such as little leagues, schools, and community improvement groups. It also provided grants to fund bricks-and-mortar type projects.

The CAP was the focal point for issues and concerns. Importantly, the process identified numerous supporters. Through the work, the company gained the endorsement of state senators and delegates, the county commission, the development authority, the local chamber of commerce, city councils, and local trade organizations, as well as many individuals. Just as important, the process identified the limited number of adversaries and their issues. For example, there were vocal detractors who were against having windmills in their view sheds or opposed to hearing the sound of the whirling blades. After a thorough review process, the Public Service Commission of West Virginia (PSC) granted US WindForce the necessary permit. The PSC stated that the project had the broadest base of support for a wind project seen by the commission. The adversaries filed an appeal with the PSC; however, the appeal was denied.

Construction has now been completed and operation has begun.

This success story illustrates how effective a CAP can be and how critical public engagement is to the final outcome. The CAP was given the information needed to develop informed decisions about the project. As a result, CAP members shared their comfort in supporting US WindForce with their families, friends, and neighbors. With the involvement of elected officials, the CAP was a powerful tool in showing the community's support to the PSC. The CAP was a key and critical ingredient in the successful effort to permit the project.

Not all efforts to site a new facility run this smoothly, particularly when public engagement isn't part of the initial permitting process. One company faced challenges when it wanted to build a new coking facility near a sprawling steel plant in western Ohio.

Company officials had counted on government relations efforts to build the necessary local support for their project. Initially, they felt this was the appropriate and only effort necessary to garner public approval.

Although the plant was supported by many civic leaders, the project faced significant opposition from a well-organized citizens group. The group used a website and media attention to build concern about the safety of the new facility, even though the federal EPA had given the company's technology the seal of approval for environmental safety. Pressure from the citizens group on the Ohio EPA and county regulator made permitting the project challenging. Media and public interest was high.

At this juncture, Ann Green Communications was brought in to assist the company in engaging the local citizens and the activist group.

After identifying key community leaders and conducting interviews with them, we established a CAP to work with the company managers throughout the permitting, construction, and operation of the new facility. We included representatives from the activist group to show the company's willingness to be open with all involved.

The activist group is a well-organized group of intelligent and dedicated individuals who earnestly didn't want the plant in their community. Led by a smart, capable woman, the group was articulate in their opposition. They clearly deserved to be at the table and participate in the process of finding common ground. This group would fall in the Fanatics category.

Initial meetings were contentious. Activists clearly did not trust company representatives. Other citizens were uncomfortable with the rancor. Ann Green Communications' skilled facilitators worked with all CAP members to build trust.

One approach was to use the CAP process to address issues presented by the activists in an open forum with media present. The result was clarification of their issues and correction of misinformation.

The CAP forum was an excellent example of True Spin. It allowed good and credible information about the project to be shared with key leaders and with media, ultimately reaching area citizens. Incorrect information was refuted. Information about the benefits of the project reached the general public. Regulators who also sat on the CAP benefited from observing that while some were unhappy about the plant being in their community, there also was public support for the permit being issued.

During construction, small incidents occurred that upset near neighbors. These issues were brought to the CAP for discussion, and corrective action was developed with all interested citizens involved.

Now that the plant is fully operational, the CAP serves as a discussion point for any issues that occur. In addition, the CAP is guiding the company in the best ways to help sustain the community. CAP members are volunteering with company representatives in reaching out to disadvantaged students in local schools. Members also conduct interviews with other citizens in the area to learn how the company can best support community needs. The survey is now an annual effort to assure that the CAP and company are addressing the correct issues and interests.

The company made the commitment to have the activist group as part of their CAP and to provide answers to their questions on a continuing basis. Their commitment serves as an example to the greater community that this company intends to be open and honest about its operations with everyone. The activist group remains an active, vital part of the plant's public engagement effort.

The role of citizens in the permitting process is good public policy. The USEPA, Army Corps of Engineers, and many state and local regulators have built in substantial opportunities for the public to take part in the process.

The important takeaway from the two examples in this chapter is that it is critical to involve the public as a partner in the permitting process from the very beginning. It is the fundamental premise of this book: when the public feels they are part of the system—and are provided the information they need to be a productive partner—the process works for everyone.

US Windforce faced stiff opposition but was able to move through the permitting process with relative ease because of the support they had garnered from the public.

The Ohio coking plant engaged citizen activists as well as other stakeholders to respond to concerns and move toward acceptance of their operations.

Remediation Sites

We have spent most of our time here talking about active manufacturing sites, but our country also is dotted with sites long abandoned, contaminated by materials that can pose a hazard to the public. Chemical plants and other operations of the past did not always manage their hazardous materials in the same careful and highly regulated way they do today.

Superfund. The word conjures images of some sort of cartoon hero. In reality, it is the federal legislation enacted in 1980 requiring the USEPA to identify, list, and clean up abandoned waste sites thought to be most dangerous to human health and the environment. The Superfund Amendments and Reauthorization Act of 1986 (SARA) reauthorized Superfund to continue cleanup activities around the country. The Emergency Planning and Community Right-to-Know Act provisions came out of SARA.

If you are of a certain age, you may remember Love Canal—a notorious Superfund site left abandoned with a toxic soup of hazardous materials blighting the land and fouling the water. It might be considered the father of the modern Superfund.

Love Canal was a community near Niagara, New York, where a hazardous waste landfill in the community created significant health problems. This one event led to the enactment of Superfund legislation. Other sites were discovered in the late 1970s, creating a national crisis.

Over the years, many of the most egregious Superfund sites have been cleaned up—or "remediated." A major challenge for the USEPA is to identify and seek out the polluters at these sites so that they might take responsibility for the damage. Then plans must be developed as to how to address the problems.

These sites can be anywhere. One such site we worked on was found adjacent to a fairway at the Pit Golf Links near Pinehurst Country Club in North Carolina. The remediation had to be conducted during the same year as the local courses were preparing to host the US Open golf tournament.

The Aberdeen Pesticide Dumps Site (APDS) included one former pesticide blending and formulating facility and four nearby areas used as dump sites for bags and boxes that once contained pesticides. The APDS was a large Superfund project, with more than a hundred thousand tons of soil to be remediated.

Aberdeen and the adjacent communities of Pinehurst and Southern Pines make up a well-known golfing and retirement area. Residents and businesspeople were frustrated with the presence of the site and with a perceived lack of communication and delays in initiating remediation. In addition, a local environmental organization, which received a Technical Assistance Grant (TAG) from the USEPA, challenged soil testing methods and identification of contaminants of concern.

Nine potentially responsible parties (PRPs) performed the work under unilateral orders from the USEPA to remediate the site. None of the PRP companies had a presence in the community.

Many technical issues related to the site complicated communications. For the soil treatment phase of the operation, the PRPs' preferred method was thermal desorption, an environmental remediation technology that uses heat to separate contaminants from soil for proper disposal. An important objective was to gain acceptance from the community for this method, which would allow millions of dollars in cost savings while effectively treating the contaminated soil.

In the groundwater design phase, the PRPs proposed to use phytoremediation, a treatment method that uses plants to mitigate an environmental problem without removal of the soil. Gaining public acceptance of this method was important because early success could mean a broader use of the method in the groundwater treatment phase, also offering the opportunity for great cost savings while achieving cleanup goals.

There were numerous community issues that had to be addressed for the cleanup to go smoothly. For example, the five areas of the site required that contaminated soil be transported on public roadways to a central treatment facility, trees and soil be removed from the property of a few neighbors of the site, and an access road and turning lane be constructed to accommodate truck traffic.

Our firm designed a comprehensive communications strategy for identifying the community's issues of concern, developing a forum for community input to the remediation process by establishing a CAP. Emphasis was placed on personal communications through meetings, informal discussions, visits to neighbors, and personal contacts with community leaders. Ongoing communications with key individuals and groups, as well as with the media, regarding the status of the remediation was critical to full public engagement.

Our staff members met with community leaders and individuals living and working near the site to clearly identify the issues of concern and to identify potential members for a CAP. The panel was established and began meetings with the PRPs to discuss key issues, such as potential impediments that could delay the cleanup, remediation technology, transportation means and routes for taking contaminated soil to a central treatment facility, and groundwater treatment design. The CAP provided input to the PRPs on these and other aspects of the cleanup and supported the companies' design plans.

We worked with the PRPs to maintain communication with the local media, with the TAG organization (which also had a representative on the CAP), and with USEPA's project manager and community outreach coordinator.

In coordination with environmental contractors working on the site, we organized an open house for the community before the soil treatment began, offering opportunity to discuss the project with PRPs and contractors, and a tour of the central treatment facility.

To keep immediate neighbors informed of the soil cleanup, we coordinated door-to-door visits as work began at each area and sent out a bimonthly letter providing updates on the cleanup. During the most active phase of soil remediation, an update was faxed each Friday to key Town of Aberdeen and Moore County officials.

In addition, a toll-free community information line was put in place as another vehicle for local citizens to get answers to their questions regarding remediation of the site. The line was answered in the office of Ann Green Communications.

All of these public engagement efforts were necessary to keep the local citizens abreast of the cleanup efforts and to be sure they had an opportunity for meaningful input into the process.

Dealing with Complications

As illustrated by the Aberdeen case study, the USEPA expects companies responsible for Superfund or other sites designated for rehabilitation to communicate to the public about the site situation, remediation plans, and any environmental or health concerns. The chemicals left to spoil the environment at these sites often are hard to identify after years of mixing with other chemicals and naturally occurring elements in the earth and groundwater. Some take years—even decades—to be remediated to a level acceptable for protection of public health. Communications can be complicated by a number of factors, including the responsible party no longer owning or operating at the site. In these situations, relationships aren't in place and must be created.

The following example shows how a company was able to build the needed relationships and support for its remediation plan even though it had left the community some years before.

As a voluntary action, a major chemical manufacturer developed measures for restoring land that held a former textiles dye plant. The company believed communicating with those who lived and worked near the site was an integral part of the program. They hired Ann Green Communications to manage the public outreach efforts.

Located adjacent to a small creek, the former textiles dye plant was located less than a mile from the center of a small town in central Virginia and covered fifty-three acres. The facility was operated by several companies between 1918 and 1986, during which time the pollution occurred. Our client bought the facility in 1980 and began dismantling it in 1986.

The contamination at the site included lead and various dyes used in clothing, such as blue jeans and socks.

As we completed our initial research, we found many issues served as challenges to positive public engagement:

∴ Former workers and other residents from the community vividly remembered, years before our client's purchase, the days of operations when few or no environmental laws existed and the plant often discharged "pink" water into the local stream.

∴ Some residents lost jobs from the manufacturing plant when it closed, and they harbored some resentment toward the company for closing the facility.

∴ Three local newspapers with circulation in the area paid close attention to environmental issues.

∴ The local congressman was very dedicated to protecting the environment.

∴ A local baseball field for little league teams also was adjacent to the site, and working to assuage concerns among parents was very important.

One of the key elements of the project was to restore the property and to donate the nonprocessing portion to the town for recreational use. This was a sensitive issue because of the contamination. Our client was committed to ensuring the community would be comfortable with the land when it was donated.

The communications program we created relied on keeping the public informed about the work. Through direct contact with community leaders, elected officials, and near neighbors, community concerns were addressed effectively and without creating public concern.

As noted, our initial research helped us understand the community issues and the media's coverage about the site. The result was a comprehensive plan that could immediately address issues important to the small town of less than six hundred residents.

Keeping immediate neighbors informed through the work included door-to-door visits as work began and when it finished. This was done to allow for all questions to be answered and any issues dealt with before the public meetings.

We created fact sheets and distributed them to neighbors and placed them in public locations to inform the community about the efforts. A toll-free number, which rang into our office, also was promoted to encourage calls if the residents wanted information.

As our client's representative, we visited offices of elected officials regularly, including the town mayor and the congressman, to keep them abreast of site activities. We provided facts about the work and the path forward to help them address any concerns.

Our client approached the project with a desire to be open about the remediation work and was committed to including key stakeholders in the process. Even though the company didn't have a long and positive history with the community, it took the necessary steps to create the needed relationships. The result was that the restoration work was successfully completed, the property was donated to the town, and the company's reputation was enhanced. Everyone gained from the experience.

Superfund on the Fast Track

Many years into the Superfund program, the USEPA determined that some of the Superfund sites were taking too long to be remediated. So they created a program to expedite certain sites: Project XL (e**X**cellence and **L**eadership), an initiative of the USEPA's Office of Reinvention.

The first XL project in the nation was located in Fairmont, West Virginia. A Fortune 100 petroleum producer, a client of Ann Green Communications, is the current owner of this former coke works. The program placed great emphasis on involving the community early in environmental projects. In addition to greater community involvement, the Project XL designation meant that the company, the USEPA, and the West Virginia Department of Environmental Protection (WVDEP) would focus on expedited plans and a quicker project completion than would likely occur under traditional procedures.

We assisted our client in forming a CAP as an integral part of the communications process. As part of the activities in recruiting community members, we conducted an open house and placed advertisements in local newspapers about the establishment of the panel. The open house also served to provide general information about the project to the community.

The panel met on a regular basis with company representatives, the USEPA, and the WVDEP. With extensive involvement of the panel, a community outreach program was implemented, including periodic direct mail to six hundred neighbors, newspaper advertisements seeking public comment, and speaking engagements with community organizations.

A key part of this outreach program involved seeking input from citizens about the needs and desires of the community regarding how the cleanup would occur and future use of the property, which had been selected as a site for an indoor water park and convention center before a decline in the economy in 2008 and tighter lending practices stalled the redevelopment project.

Perhaps most important, the company maintained their status as a committed and responsible corporate citizen.

Many corporations have been frustrated in managing remediation projects. They often are required to clean up messes left by former owners and/or made years before, when environmental regulations were less stringent and protective. The remediation processes are expensive and certainly don't add a penny to the bottom line. Yet, by utilizing the True Spin philosophy of honest communication with the public, companies can complete their obligations efficiently and without damage to their reputations.

Chapter Six *True Spin* Takeaways

∴ Public participation is an important, often essential, part of the permitting process.

∷ It is easier to engage your stakeholders outside of a contentious situation.

∷ Remediation efforts need public participation programs to be successful.

∷ Good outreach regarding remediation activities include:

○ assessing community members' attitudes and understanding regarding sites in their neighborhoods

○ establishing, facilitating, and administering community outreach forums such as CAPs, working groups, and public availability sessions to provide information and gain input from stakeholders

○ developing and using various communications vehicles (fact sheets, call-in information line, email contact address, etc.) to inform citizens and to provide them access

○ developing and maintaining communications with elected officials, environmental advocates, the media, and other special audiences

○ continuing these communications strategies until the last day of the cleanup effort

CHAPTER SEVEN

Environmental Justice

Whether the disadvantaged population is from a blighted urban setting or poor Appalachian area, whether there is a racial component or not, environmental justice is an emerging issue that can be the difference between your organization being welcomed to the community or shunned and shut down.

The USEPA defines environmental justice as "the fair and meaningful treatment of all people regardless of race, color, national origin, or income with respect to the development, implementation, and enforcement of environmental laws, regulations, and policies." USEPA further states, "Fair treatment means no group of people should bear a disproportionate share of the negative environmental consequences resulting from industrial, governmental, and commercial operations or policies."

As part of their guidance to industry, the USEPA stipulates that disadvantaged groups must be involved in the conversation in a meaningful way. The agency labels this "meaningful involvement" and further describes it as:

- People have an opportunity to participate in decisions about activities that may affect their environment.

- The public's contribution can influence the regulatory agency's decision.

- Community concerns will be considered in the decision-making process.

- Decision makers will seek out and facilitate the involvement of those potentially affected.

In 2014, the USEPA developed their initial guidance regarding how to recognize and respond to environmental justice situations. It stipulated how and when to conduct enhanced outreach to communities where permit or permit renewals were scheduled. Significant in the guidance was the requirement that business and industry must "engage neighboring communities to build trust and promote better understanding."

In 2016, they created a strategic plan, EJ 2020, providing a roadmap to where they see the future of environmental justice. They envision that environmental justice will be integrated into everything they do and that environmental justice will be routinely considered in permitting. This means that USEPA permit writers will consider whether there are environmental justice concerns present in the community affected by the permit. In communities they deem as likely overburdened, they may conduct extra research and, based on that, "establish appropriate permit terms and conditions to address environmental justice concerns to the extent supported by the relevant information and law."

As part of the environmental justice initiative, USEPA created an Environmental Justice Academy to help citizens become more involved. This is a nine-month training program to give participants the skills they can use "to identify and address environmental challenges in their communities."

The academy was started in September 2015 and includes lectures on topics such as "how to leverage human, social, intellectual, technical, legal, and financial resources to make long-term progress in a community" and "how to use consensus-building processes and skills to help ensure successful collaboration and negotiations."

The first graduates completed the course in May 2016.

Regulators at the USEPA want state and local regulators to actively work to identify environmental justice issues and conduct permitting with those issues in mind. The goal is to have communities burdened by environmental justice issues to be able to be their own advocates.

It is a noble goal to reduce the disparities in environmental outcomes among communities based on who lives there. The program clearly is aimed at giving a voice to those who may not have been heard when decisions affecting their environment were made in the past. These goals also emphasize the very premise of True Spin—and of this book—that you need to truly engage with your stakeholders in order to be successful.

In September 2004, a cement company had been working to build a state-of-the-art cement grinding facility in the Waterfront South area of Camden, New Jersey. The area had been blighted by years of industrial use, then decay. Many of the homes in that area of Camden had been abandoned to drug dealers and other societal challenges. A hardy group of citizens was trying desperately to improve the living conditions of those citizens still there. When a new company wanted to build a cement grinding facility, some of them felt that one more industrial neighbor was the last thing they wanted or needed.

The Waterfront South community had suffered decades-long frustration with industry polluting their area. Mounds of rusted metal were stacked along roadways. Abandoned sites of rusted columns and tattered buildings were positioned next to whole blocks left to nature's whim.

Leaders of the community had felt the sting of racial and environmental injustice for a long time. Many good and sincere people had tried to stem the decline, with limited success. Efforts were underway in a few neighborhoods—primarily led by local religious leaders—to tear down abandoned houses and revitalize businesses in the area. One local minister, a gentleman from South Carolina, ran a number of programs to help disadvantaged youth get a high school diploma or GED. It was clearly an uphill battle that left bitter feelings. Many felt they weren't being listened to, and they weren't even sure who should be listening. So when the cement company wanted to build a new plant, all the residents saw was yet another polluting entity adding to an already overburdened community. During the public meetings for the permitting process for the new plant, citizens filled with the years of anger and frustration over not being heard organized a revolt.

The company had spent thousands of dollars in legal fees to try to get the permit to build and operate a state-of-the-art facility in what had clearly been a highly industrialized area. The opposition to their plant caught the company by surprise. At this juncture, legal counsel for the company asked Ann Green Communications for our advice. What our research uncovered was that the company hadn't understood that their plant represented to the folks of Waterfront South the proverbial "straw that broke the camel's back." It was their red line in the sand—they didn't want another industrial facility in their area, period. Public hearings that had been held by regulators only served to reinforce the opposition to the plant. A previous attempt at a community panel had not been sustained.

Once the company better understood the problem, they agreed to try again to engage the public in dialogue sessions. They allowed us to organize a community advisory panel for the citizens and representatives of the company to discuss their positions face-to-face, with the goal of reaching a compromise acceptable to both sides. Members came from the local churches and social service agencies. They included teachers and community organizers. From time to time, regulators from the New Jersey Department of Environmental Protection attended the meetings.

Early meetings of the Camden group were contentious. Frustrated by the years of neglect, the neighbors were hostile. Some raised the specter of racism, asserting that the minority community was overburdened because it was predominantly African-American. Others were concerned about high rates of asthma among the children in the area and associated those with industrial pollution. The advisory panel setting allowed residents to vent those frustrations, but it also allowed the company to explain what they were trying to accomplish, including the technology they were using to limit emissions. The company explained that they were going to bring badly needed jobs and would prioritize the hiring of local workers. The company emphasized that they also wanted to be a supporting partner with the neighborhood.

After nearly a year of meetings and building understanding and—slowly—trust, the company was allowed to construct and operate their plant. The plant committed to hiring locally and working with local civic and philanthropic organizations to improve community conditions. With the CAP's guidance, the plant developed programs with local schools to provide scholarships for deserving students, helped local groups fund summer camps for underprivileged children, and worked with other groups to build and sustain programs to improve housing, create community gardens, and clean up vacant lots and streets.

The hardest part about public participation programs is that they require people who often don't like to engage in public discourse to do just that. Often trained as engineers, plant managers or other authorities at a facility are often not comfortable or trained to deal with angry citizens. Plant managers' brains may not be wired to deal with the emotional side of community interaction. The people in the Waterfront South part of Camden were demonstrably angry and determined to stop the plant. The plant manager was a good, decent man and a capable leader, but he did not like confrontations with emotional people making what to him were illogical arguments. It was only after he was able to listen to them in the advisory panel setting that he could fully understand the situation and make persuasive arguments in response.

Once the plant manager heard directly and personally from the citizens, he understood where they were coming from. He responded with empathy and presented arguments that helped the citizens see that he was willing to become a partner with them—not an adversary. In return, the citizens were more open to hearing about the plant's efforts to be a good neighbor. As a result, they were less vocal in their opposition to the plant coming into their neighborhood.

In the end, everyone gained from the experience. The citizens gained a new partner in sustaining their community, and the plant was able to gain its operating permit and employ local people in well-paying jobs.

Finding Common Ground

Another example of the power of public engagement in addressing environmental justice challenges can be found in southern Ohio. A chemical plant situated near Cincinnati had been operating on the site for decades as a privately owned soap manufacturing plant without engaging the many near neighbors of the facility.

The largest neighborhood near the facility was a low-income housing development across the street. This predominantly African-American development had high unemployment and crime. The residents' relationship to the plant was one of fear of a release or explosion from which they couldn't escape.

In 1993, things began to change. As a result of the decision by the owners of the plant to meet the guidelines of the Chemical Manufacturers Association (now American Chemistry Council) calling for ongoing dialogue with site neighbors, Ann Green Communications was asked to help them form a CAP.

After visiting with local citizens in all the surrounding towns, we found a great disparity among the demographic groups of the area. Most of the plant sits in the middle class city of St. Bernard. The nearest neighbors, however, live in a predominantly minority low-income housing development just across the highway from the plant. Membership in the CAP had to include key leaders from both neighborhoods, which felt worlds apart. Our research found the housing complex had a well-organized group of leaders dedicated to the residents. Including those leaders in the process would be critical to successful engagement. We were determined to bring the different groups together to find common ground.

Neighbors from St. Bernard were mostly supportive of the plant's economic contributions to the area, while some were concerned about environmental emissions. Citizens from the Cincinnati side, the low-income housing development, were mostly concerned about their personal safety. Early discussions focused on understanding the shortcomings in all these areas and developing an approach to dealing with each that would be acceptable to all the CAP members.

The CAP's first priority was on outreach to neighbors about how to shelter in place should a chemical release occur from any of the many potential sources in the area. They also wanted to provide materials and education for local schools in emergency response procedures. The CAP proved to be an excellent catalyst in bringing local emergency responders who sat on the CAP together with the neighbors to improve citizens' awareness of what to do in an emergency. It also

improved the trust level between the responders and this constituency. Ultimately, the pilot program in the local schools
spread across the entire area.

In addition, at each meeting, the plant managers
discussed what they were doing to reduce emissions and
improve the plant's safety record. Representatives from city,
county, and state regulatory agencies attended CAP meetings
to discuss how they were working to improve the environment. Over the more than two decades the CAP has been
meeting, members have seen significant reduction in environmental emissions.

The CAP continues today. Much of the effort now is
to continue to build on the foundation of the early years.
In addition, the plant sponsors local teachers to education
conferences and helps civic groups meet the needs of local
children through tutoring and after-school programs.

Environmental justice is a real and ever-present issue
in many communities. Companies need to recognize the
concerns whether they feel they have added to the community's burden or not. Those that engage in candid dialogue
with their neighbors have the best chance of being accepted
into the community. Neighborhoods that recognize that
some companies want to be sincere partners with them can
benefit greatly from welcoming them. It's about using True
Spin to achieve gain-gain.

Chapter Seven *True Spin* Takeaways

⁘ Environmental justice is the "fair and meaningful treatment of all people regardless of race, color, national origin, or income with respect to development, implementation, and enforcement of environmental laws, regulations, and policies." —USEPA

⁘ The USEPA has been aggressive in helping communities identify and respond to environmental justice issues.

⁘ Sound principles of public engagement apply in communities where environmental justice may be in play just as much as in any other community.

CHAPTER EIGHT

Building Sustainable Communities

In chapter 5, we introduced you to the Mosaic Company, a company we have worked with for several years. Mosaic operates phosphate mines in central Florida, extracting the phosphate rock from the unique formations found there. Phosphate is an essential ingredient in fertilizer, and without fertilizer it would be impossible to grow enough food for the world's people. Their slogan, "We Feed the World," then, is fitting.

In 2009, Mosaic issued its first sustainability report and has shown significant improvement since then. The report captures the many initiatives Mosaic has undertaken to protect the environment, reduce water consumption, and help farmers grow more crops to feed the world. Neil Beckingham, who managed their sustainability effort out of Mosaic's Environmental and Regulatory Affairs Department, is an engaging Australian and excellent communicator who loves to share what Mosaic has done to improve the world, one community at a time. He regularly visits the company's many community advisory panels to give a report card on how Mosaic is doing in meeting its obligations as a world-class company. He always has a very good story to tell.

Mosaic, which Neil describes as being a best-in-class company that values the triple bottom line of people, planet, and profit, believes in sustainability. The company is committed to its employees and to the communities in which it operates, including supporting better nutrition. As an employer, it wants to be first to be chosen, a strong business partner, and a significant economic driver. Finally, its leaders recognize their responsibility as stewards of the environment and the need to work toward energy and resource efficiency.

Mosaic is involved in many programs for accomplishing environmental goals, including significantly reducing its carbon footprint and slashing the amount of water it uses. It has developed ways to manufacture fertilizer that allow farmers to use less for the same results, and it works with farmers to show them ways to apply fertilizer more efficiently. These initiatives are good for farmers, good for people who will benefit from the crops, and good for the environment.

In a unique initiative, Mosaic has partnerships in third-world countries to help the local farmers learn to grow more food on less land—land that is at a premium in some areas.

In Florida, Mosaic is at the forefront in "food security" efforts—working to meet challenges in making sure people have enough to eat. The company sponsors an annual statewide symposium on reducing hunger and works with the local food bank to supply children who depend on school lunches for their daily nutrition with food to take home for the weekends.

What Mosaic does very well is to focus on what matters most to the community and then engage its neighbors in solving those issues.

Many companies are active in their communities. They may encourage their employees to participate in charity activities, or they may financially support United Way or Relay for Life. What sets some programs apart is that their work is driven by public engagement. They start with a needs assessment with their stakeholders and build programs to respond to those needs.

Remember the story about Rockhouse Lake in chapter 3? With input from their community, Arch Coal determined that one major problem in the area was lack of recreational facilities to keep young people off drugs and out of trouble. The idea of developing the lake was a natural progression out of discussions with the company's neighbors.

Let's look at an example where a company's charitable giving fell short of its goal. A large refining company operating in a medium-sized city had for a number of years given the bulk of its philanthropic budget to the city's symphony. In and of itself, an annual gift to help sustain the arts is a good thing. The problem was that the refinery was located in a lower-income community and none of the budget for charitable giving was directed toward helping the refinery's nearest neighbors. There were many worthwhile programs in the company's community that deserved support. It wasn't until the refinery managers started meeting regularly with their neighbors because of complaints about odors that they learned that the lack of support for this disadvantaged neighborhood was a real issue. It took facing one problem to identify another. Over time, the company's managers and their neighbors learned to discuss their issues and have worked toward building meaningful relationships. The refinery now supports a local community center and other worthwhile activities in its own backyard.

Inviting your stakeholders to help you administer your philanthropic budget does not take the decision making out of your hands—it's just sound management. It allows you to vet your list of donations with your key stakeholders and gives you an excuse to refuse requests that don't support your primary community.

Helping sustain your community builds bridges to your closest stakeholders that are hard to tear down. By giving a little, you can gain a lot. Everyone gains when you help your community in ways that really matter. It's not the size of the effort but how directly the effort impacts the target audience that matters most.

Education is most often the number-one target of industrial philanthropic budgets, and for good reason. Supporting education is good business and comes with an amazing list of positives. Directly supporting schools leads to better schools for your children and your employees' children. Having better schools makes it easier to recruit better employees to your area and means you are taking the first steps in raising capable employees for the future. Supporting schools means you will receive the gratitude of the vast majority of your stakeholders.

Public participation in your educational efforts can maximize what you accomplish. Find out what your neighbors believe are the most pressing priorities. Identify partners that can use your help. A wide range of possibilities exist, from providing mini-grants to individual classrooms for science projects, to sponsoring school events like science fairs, to sending teachers to symposiums and covering their classes while they attend. All can be part of a meaningful sustainability program and can help build relationships with your stakeholders that last a generation.

Proactive Workforce Development

The need for an available workforce is something that industry across the country continues to face as aging employees retire. One roadblock to workforce development is the notion many students and parents have that one must go to college to be successful.

Industry, educators, and the community recognized this in South Charleston, West Virginia, and decided it was time to build a collaborative effort to introduce the facts. The mission was to create an awareness of the opportunities in industry, with a specific focus on careers that do not require a four-year degree. They wanted parents and students to know that industry jobs are available and come with a great starting salary, benefits, and an opportunity for career growth. Their intent was to reach students from kindergarten through high school and their parents.

Together with a group of community stakeholders, industry developed a program to provide annual grants to support math and science in each local school. Fun, hands-on experiments were made available to the schools to bring math and science to life.

To emphasize the message to parents, industry and community representatives sponsored an "Industry, Education, and Community Night." Hosted at the area's career and technical college, the event brought together students and educators from the elementary, middle, and high school levels, alongside representatives of industry, the college, and career and vocational schools, to further participants' understanding of the benefits of a career in industry.

Just about every manufacturing facility, every industrial entity, has some kind of philanthropic budget. What you do with those resources, large or small, makes all the difference.

Don't guess what matters to your stakeholders. Ask them. Engage them in the process. Make whatever you do count to the stakeholders.

Chapter Eight *True Spin* Takeaways

∵ The best companies take building sustainability into their cultures very seriously.

∵ Helping to build strong communities where you operate is a cornerstone of gain-gain. Everyone wins.

∵ Public participation can play a major role in successful sustainability efforts.

CHAPTER NINE

Public Engagement during a Crisis

A twelve-inch pipe ruptured at a large chemical plant in the Florida panhandle, and over the next twenty minutes, thirty thousand pounds of a pungent mixture was released. On a summer evening in Florida, the smell of rotten fish wafted through the heavy air.

Flaws in the initial response to the emergency created more problems. The county's system, designed to call close residents, called some but not all of the plant's neighbors. A major US highway was blocked for several hours. Neighbors called the plant and clogged emergency lines. Some neighbors were improperly evacuated; others appropriately sheltered in place.

An incident at the plant affecting the community is a plant manager's nightmare. However, thanks to public engagement, this story had a positive outcome.

We managed an active CAP for them. The group of twenty-five neighbors had been providing a sounding board for the plant's initiatives and helped the plant understand community concerns. Within hours of the incident, we brought the CAP members together in an emergency session. Panel members included environmental leaders as well as near neighbors, civic leaders, and emergency responders. They sprang into action, helping disseminate information to the public about the accident through word of mouth and in their newsletter, which we developed for them. We also helped them organize and host a special public meeting to allow concerned citizens to speak directly with plant managers.

In addition to CAP activities, a phone bank was set up to answer neighbors' questions about health care and insurance issues related to the foul smell in homes and cars. The phones were manned twenty-four hours a day for the first seventy-two hours after the incident, during which time plant employees responded to 180 calls.

At the recommendation of the CAP, the plant sent employees in teams of two to visit the nearest neighbors. The employees distributed a letter of apology from the plant manager along with a shelter-in-place how-to video previously created by the CAP and an emergency response pamphlet. This personal contact was designed to help neighbors understand that plant workers were concerned about what had happened and were willing to listen to neighbors' issues. The workers visited 834 homes and talked directly with 435 families in a three-day period.

Neighbors were very responsive to the plant's efforts to reach out to them. The local newspapers praised the plant's sensitivity and immediate responsiveness in editorials. The plant and CAP worked with local emergency responders to improve emergency notification, and the plant installed sirens at their fence line to alert immediate neighbors of an incident.

Relationships as Insurance

Crises can happen at any time and come in all sizes and shapes. They are unplanned events that have the potential to significantly disrupt operations. A crisis can impact a company's credibility or pose a significant health, environmental, economic, or legal liability.

In industrial settings, the most likely crisis scenarios involve an environmental incident, an accident, or a regulatory or labor issue. They might be prompted by natural disasters or product recall. More recently, workplace violence and acts of terror have been added to the list.

In our fast-paced, media-driven world, a crisis can be prompted by negative media coverage, including on social media. At a coal mine in Virginia, for example, workers experienced runaway social media. The mine was about to tell some of its workers they would be laid off. One of the mine's supervisors told his wife ahead of time, and she in turn posted the news on her Facebook page *before* those to be laid off were informed.

In a more egregious example, the spokesperson for a regulatory agency announced the name of a deceased worker from an industrial accident before the family was notified of the tragedy. Very unfortunately, the family members heard about the fatality on the local news.

There are many consequences of a crisis. Of course, the first consideration is and should be the human toll. Businesses also must be cognizant of the economic loss, legal liabilities, and regulatory actions. A major consequence of a significant crisis is damage to reputation, and for the manager in charge at the time of a crisis, it has the potential to stall a career or even kill it.

Most of us purchase insurance to protect us in a crisis at home. At work, we probably have similar policies that protect plant equipment and provide legal support if needed. What about an insurance policy for dealing with an angry public in the aftermath of an issue? If you have developed a public engagement program, you have just that—insurance in the form of relationships you have built with your community stakeholders that can help you get through a difficult situation.

The scenario of the pipe rupture at the plant in Florida cited at the beginning of this chapter is a good example of how a plant was able to draw on the existing goodwill of much of its community to see it through a difficult situation.

What if you don't have those relationships ahead of time and you have an accident or issue affecting the community? Let's look at two contrasting examples—one in which the outreach was effective and another in which, shall we say, the jury is still out.

On a cold morning in early January 2014, residents of Charleston and South Charleston, West Virginia, noticed an unusual odor in the air that smelled of rancid licorice. Within hours, the odor was emanating from faucets and toilets in homes and businesses up and down the Kanawha Valley. Our office sits in downtown South Charleston. When I got out of my car at the office, the odor that hit me was strong and unpleasant.

A company that stored crude MCHM, a chemical used in the coal industry, had a breach of a storage tank. The material flowed out of the tank, easily traversed a crumbling dike, and ended its journey in the Elk River near an intake for the drinking water supply for the local water company.

It wasn't until much later in the day that the residents of the area understood what we were experiencing, and then information was scant and trickled out to the public. According to press accounts, it took six hours for the water company to make a statement to the media and thirty hours before the company that leaked the material faced reporters.

Little was known about the health effects of ingesting or coming in contact with the chemical. The executive director of the Kanawha Charleston Health Department said, "The fact is, we are unwilling participants of a live human experiment." People were scared about what they didn't know and angry about what they had to endure.

The governor of West Virginia issued a ban to citizens in several counties: "Don't drink, cook with, or bathe in the water." Ultimately, an estimated three hundred thousand homes and businesses were without the use of their water for drinking, cooking, and—in the case of small children and elderly—bathing. Water restrictions applied to customers in a nine-county area. It would be nine days before customers were told they could safely use the water. Schools were canceled for a week but had to use bottled water until the end of February.

Because of the problem, most of the restaurants in the area had to close, and many businesses sent employees home. Local businesses lost an estimated $61 million in revenue during the event.

Eventually, state and federal officials joined the water company in response efforts. Testing and flushing procedures were initiated by the water company. Citizens were told to flush their water systems to remove any remaining residue of the chemical.

Media coverage was extensive, but social media drove the issue. Twitter and Facebook were rampant with the latest, sometimes inaccurate, information.

Adding to the negativity of the situation, the offending company was not forthcoming with information in a timely manner, and the water company didn't fully understand what it was dealing with until hours into the event. The public was left to guess what was causing the odor for far too long.

Ramifications of the situation continue. Multiple lawsuits have been filed. New regulations for above-ground storage tanks have been passed by the West Virginia legislature. Concern about the location and management of the water intake remain.

As attested by comments in the local newspaper gripe line, no one came out of this situation looking particularly good in the eyes of the public. The incident was later labeled by the National Science Foundation's William Cooper as "one of the largest human-made environmental disasters in this century."

The public has not been well served during this crisis. Citizens have not been invited to be part of the process in any meaningful way. Credibility of the companies involved was damaged and trust was not built.

As a consequence of not engaging the public—not being forthcoming with timely and meaningful information—the companies involved are suffering major financial ramifications. The cost of the combined legal settlements, at this writing, has reached more that $150 million.

The Power of Effective Outreach

Can public engagement make a significant difference in the outcome of a substantial crisis? Here is an example of how it certainly helped.

On October 11, 2000, the coal sludge impoundment for Martin County Coal in Inez, Kentucky, broke, sending several tons of sludge careening down the mountainside and into creeks, rivers, and homes along its path. As a result, national and regional media descended on the mine management for answers. So did the thousands of residents affected by the sludge, as did environmental activist groups, which labeled it the worst ecological disaster in memory.

Ann Green Communications was called upon to lend assistance in managing the media calls and to support the company's efforts in responding to the needs of its neighbors who had been affected.

Our consultants worked with representatives of Martin County Coal to respond to all media inquiries in a timely manner. Several agencies from the federal government and the states of Kentucky and Ohio were involved in the issue (Ohio because the sludge reached its rivers). Even the Coast Guard was involved. A joint information center was established so that all information from the disaster would be coordinated among the interested parties, including the mine and state and local disaster relief agencies and regulators.

Media interviews were set up to meet the needs of media while recognizing the mine president's need to manage the disaster. Videotape for local television stations was prepared for those who were not allowed onto the site because of security issues. Once the site was secured, media were brought in for a guided tour.

Within a few days of the event, we organized community meetings at local churches and community buildings around the area. We facilitated dialogue among the residents, mine representatives, and government agencies, working with them to identify outstanding issues and develop opportunities for resolution. Many of the issues regarding needs for water, water well examination, and sludge removal were managed through these meetings. The meetings showed the people of the area that the mine regretted the accident, cared about their situations, and wanted to help. The people were angry at first, but many came to accept the outreach meetings as evidence that the company was trying to do the right thing.

We created fact sheets and distributed them throughout the communities to keep residents apprised of cleanup efforts and erected displays of the cleanup efforts in key local gathering points as the work progressed.

Because we met the needs of media, reporting was generally fair and balanced. Martin County Coal received accolades for its quick response to the emergency and media accessibility.

Through our outreach meetings, we were able to identify community needs. People needing water had it delivered to their door whenever possible. Some people were relocated to hotels. Others received a free evaluation of their water, set up through the health department by the mining company.

Throughout the extensive cleanup efforts, we worked hard to keep the public and media informed of progress and challenges as they arose.

Crisis Communication Plans

Virtually all industrial facilities have an emergency response plan; few have a crisis communications plan. A crisis communications plan allows you to tap into the goodwill you have within your community. For example, the near neighbors who worked with the Florida plant called the plant managers when they heard rumors in the community about the pipe rupture. This allowed the managers to reach out and respond before misinformation became fact.

The best crisis communications plans are developed *with* your key stakeholders. Engaging your neighbors in planning is an excellent way to build new relationships or improve existing ones. Citizens want to know the risks you pose and what you do to reduce those risks. They want to understand how you would respond should an incident occur. If community leaders are included in your planning process, they can offer invaluable guidance.

In the Kanawha Valley in West Virginia, birthplace of the petrochemical industry, members of the community met together with the emergency responders and elected officials to create comprehensive plans. They worked to ensure that local residents knew how to shelter in place should the need arise. During emergency response drills, community members served as observers and helped identify deficiencies in the communications process.

A great example of community-industry partnership can be found in a small western Kentucky town where several industrial facilities are located. The plants decided two decades ago to engage the public in ongoing dialogue about their plant activities. Working with local community stakeholders, they created a system for community alert long before such systems were commonplace. Together, they researched community alert systems and chose alarms and telephone calling services that met their needs. They also disseminated flyers with details of the new plans and developed a program to assure that children in local schools know what to do in an emergency. They continue to hold an annual community meeting—drawing up to two thousand residents—to reinforce the plans they carefully put in place many years ago.

In both of these cases, the relationships served both the industry and the public in challenging times. Better understanding, open communications, and solid communications plans can make all the difference.

Chapter Nine *True Spin* Takeaways

∵ Having the support of your key stakeholders during a crisis is critical to long-term success.

∵ Initiating public engagement during a crisis is challenging but can be rewarding.

CONCLUSION

Public Engagement Is the Newest Technology

More people get their news from small, handheld devices than from any other source. Friends often text rather than talk to one another when they are in the same room. Coffee shops are filled with patrons engrossed in laptops. So why would the next generation of industrial leaders feel the need to talk to someone face-to-face? Because electronic communication can't replace the need for the human connection.

Industry is often seen as a "gray corporate wall," devoid of empathy and caring. The only thing that matters is making a profit. In research we conducted for one client seeking input on a potential initiative, one citizen opined, "Don't corporations have a heart anymore?" To many, the phrase "good corporate citizen" is an oxymoron. However, we believe that, increasingly, the manager who can break down that gray corporate wall and show the human side of business will be a star. That requires an ability to communicate clearly and with compassion with people who may not trust you.

Public engagement is a bottom-line function. As I have tried to illustrate, the willingness to have a dialogue with the public—to listen to their hopes and concerns—is key to building credibility. Credibility is the first step toward being trusted. When industry has earned the public's trust, it can move forward with its initiatives. The chemical plant gains a permit to build a new unit. The cement plant is welcomed into a new community. The company trying to remediate an old production site gains approval for their plan. The mine has the support of its neighbors during challenging times.

Managers who embrace their responsibility to engage their stakeholders in meaningful dialogue also gain great value for their efforts. They obtain the necessary guidance from key constituencies to achieve their goals, be it a new permit or support for other plans. They gain value in time saved because they can concentrate their precious time into a few community meetings rather than many individual ones. They have the potential to save a great deal of money if they are able to achieve their goals with the support of the public rather than spending thousands of dollars in legal fees defending their actions against community-driven lawsuits.

Managers who follow the philosophy that the bottom line is all that matters usually project that attitude. Rarely is the public fooled. The manager may talk a good game, but people are savvy when it comes to honesty and integrity. The public can spot a phony a mile away. They will challenge your very right to operate if they believe you are being dishonest or untrustworthy.

Accept the public as a legitimate partner. Involve them in your decisions whenever possible. Listen to their concerns and try to address them. Try to understand how they feel—fear, anger, or confusion. Be honest, frank, and open. Speak clearly and with compassion. Be accountable for your words and actions.

Companies that hire and keep managers who follow these basic rules of engagement with the public become highly respected members of the communities in which they operate. They are considered excellent places to work. They make positive contributions to their cities and towns. In turn, they are supported and encouraged to thrive. The managers are successful, and the company's bottom line is fed.

Public engagement is not public relations. The two terms are not interchangeable. PR is a one-way street. Put your facts out there and hope they stick. Push your messages through the filter of the media to your key audiences. Publish brochures and the like to get your messages out.

Our premise from the beginning of this book is that educating the public about your operations isn't enough—that way of thinking is outdated. Engaging your key stakeholders, be they employees, near neighbors, local elected officials, environmental activists, or other opinion leaders, in ongoing dialogue is true public engagement: True Spin.

Knowing how to engage the public takes knowledge and skill. Just as you need an environmental engineer for a complex remediation project or a lawyer for a legal problem, you need an expert in the field of public engagement to guide you.

Traditional PR firms may fail to fully understand the nuances of building strong relationships at the grassroots level. They are experts in media relations and event planning but may not have the knowledge and experience to guide you through the process of establishing meaningful and lasting relationships with your key audiences. They are often generalists and may not know the intricacies of your industry. They may be consulting for a hospital one day and a dry cleaner the next.

In-house PR professionals fully understand your business but are hampered by being from the inside for three reasons. First, their livelihood depends on satisfying the company leadership, which means they may have trouble challenging that leadership when they believe the wrong path is being taken. Second, they probably don't have the breadth of experience, gained from working on a variety of challenging scenarios, to provide all the guidance you need. Third, they cannot serve the role of mediator between their own company and the public, because everyone knows where their loyalty lies. Conflict can easily arise because the in-house mediator can't provide a buffer that a third-party negotiator can.

Creating and leading successful public engagement initiatives requires a unique set of skills. The facilitators/negotiators must be good communicators and be able to skillfully interact with a wide variety of individuals with varying levels of education and life experiences. They must genuinely want all engaged in the process—both the company and the community—to gain from the experience. They must be able to help both sides see the value in the process. They must have experience in a wide variety of situations to be able to recognize and navigate through potential pitfalls. They must be familiar with the basic operations of the industry they are trying to help and have a working knowledge of the regulations governing the industry.

For engineers and other technically trained managers, sharing control with a nontechnical public may seem like the worst idea ever. It may not seem logical. Yet sharing control through public engagement allows you to gain so much—the confidence of your neighbors, the respect of your peers, and the appreciation of your corporation for a job well done. It's actually one of the most logical moves you can make.

True Spin Takeaways

❖ Public engagement is a bottom-line function for industries with environmental, health, and safety challenges.

❖ Public engagement can break down "gray corporate walls."

❖ Nothing replaces human interaction, particularly at the community level.

❖ Accept the public as a legitimate partner. Listen to them. Involve them in your decisions wherever possible.

❖ Great value can be derived from a public engagement effort done correctly.

❖ Knowing how to effectively engage the public takes knowledge, experience, and skill. Use an expert to guide you.

ABOUT THE AUTHOR

Ann S. Green is founder and president of Ann Green Communications and is a nationally recognized leader in public engagement regarding environmental, health, and safety issues.

Ann has more than thirty-five years of experience consulting with over a hundred companies across the United States. She was instrumental in developing community advisory panels (CAPs), which provide two-way communication between businesses and their stakeholders, including the public. Ann has facilitated community dialogue forums and provides stakeholder relationship counseling and media interview and communications training for clients in the chemical, petroleum, electric and wind energy, coal and phosphate mining, cement, and paper industries.

Ann has worked with major coal companies in pioneering comprehensive crisis management plans for the industry. She also has developed international crisis management plans for the chemical industry.

Before founding Ann Green Communications in 1991, she was president of the Chemical and Environmental Affairs Division of a regional public relations firm based in Charleston, West Virginia. In addition, she has taught public relations and journalism at the college level.

Ann has earned a master's degree in journalism and behavioral science from West Virginia University and a bachelor's degree in history and journalism from Glenville State College. She was honored as Practitioner of the Year by the West Virginia Chapter of the Public Relations Society of America and received that organization's Lifetime Achievement Award. She was recognized by the Charleston-area YWCA as a Woman of Achievement and was a finalist for West Virginia Entrepreneur of the Year, sponsored by Ernst and Young. In 2012, she was honored by Glenville State College as Alumna of the Year.

ABOUT ANN GREEN COMMUNICATIONS

Ann Green Communications enables our clients to build open and honest relationships with stakeholders through effective communication strategies. Our philosophy and business approach are based on the importance of building relationships between business clients and their stakeholders. We apply this philosophy nationwide and deliver results for all involved—companies and the communities in which they operate. We produce solutions for many of the most recognized companies in the world. Our team works across the nation and with international clients to ensure business objectives are met by building effective communication strategies.

Our programs are designed to establish trust and collaboration, allowing issues to be addressed in a manner that leads to success. In the current regulatory environment, industry needs the support of stakeholders—from elected officials and community leaders to near neighbors. Our strategies are the road map to make that happen.

After being in business for over twenty-five years, no challenge is new to us—including siting new facilities, working to secure construction and operating permits, calming fears, and responding to industrial crises. The emphasis of our work in all situations is to create greater understanding.

Known nationally for our public engagement programs, including community advisory panels (CAPs), we also develop complex communications solutions for environmental, health, and safety issues, including remediation sites.

We apply our knowledge of the many dimensions of relationship management to assist a variety of business sectors. Our work enables our clients to effectively engage their stakeholders.

We have a passion for our work. We want our clients to make the most of every communication opportunity to allow them to thrive in a trusting and sustaining environment.

Please visit our website at www.anngreencomm.com or contact us at (800) 784-4343.

SERVICES

Ann Green has over thirty-five years of experience as a communications consultant and facilitator. Her services include:

- ⁘ Environmental Health and Safety Communications

- ⁘ Engaging Communities

- ⁘ Community Advisory Panels

- ⁘ Site Remediation Communications

- ⁘ Crisis Planning Counseling

- ⁘ Communications Training

- ⁘ Media Interview Training

- Presentation Training

- Executive Training

- Public Relations and Issues Advertising

phone: 1.800.784.4343

website: www.annsgreen.com

email: ann@annsgreen.com